This book will save you thousands of dollars on the purchase of your next new vehicle. It will give you an advantage when dealing with salespeople because I plan to take you "inside" the business. There are seven easy steps to follow that I've outlined. Follow them and you'll benefit greatly .

My qualifications for writing this book are many. I've been involved in every facet of the automobile business during the past 20 years. I've sold cars off lots, bought cars for lots, appraised them, detailed them, and sold new cars and trucks at dealerships. I have had almost every title in an automobile dealership that you can have, from Porter to General Manager. I have arbitrated several *Lemon Law* complaints for both the manufacturer and the State of Texas. I am a member of both the Society of Professional Sales Counselors and the Society of Professional Sales Managers. I have managed all of the Sales, Finance, Service, Fleet, Parts, Rental, Leasing Departments including the Body Shop and the General Offices at some of the largest automobile dealerships in the world.

There are secrets, gimmicks, cons, ploys and facts you need to be aware of when purchasing a new vehicle. I'll tell you all of them. Yes, reading this book could easily save you thousands of dollars and much headache and heartache. You'll be better able to negotiate with dealers and sales-persons on your next new car, truck, or van purchase.

Cliff Evans

HOW TO BUY A NEW CAR

AND SAVE THOU$ANDS

HOW TO BUY A NEW CAR
AND SAVE THOU$ANDS

OR

THE BOOK YOUR AUTOMOBILE DEALER HOPES YOU NEVER READ!

by

Cliff Evans

SWAN Publishing
Texas ✱ California ✱ New York

Author: Cliff Evans
Editor/Publisher: Pete Billac
Cover Design: Renee Ruscoe
Layout Design: Sharon Davis

HOW TO BUY A NEW CAR and Save Thou$ands is available in quantity discounts through SWAN Publishing Company, 126 Live Oak, Alvin, TX 77511 (713) 388-2547 or FAX (713) 585-3738.

Printed in the United States of America.

Dedication

To Candy and Clifton, my loving children.

FOREWORD

Have you, like most of the buying public, gone to an automobile dealership and felt helpless, intimidated, or even a bit frightened of the salespeople; like a minnow in a school of sharks? If you don't know what you're doing, you should feel a little queasy because without knowing the "inner workings" of a dealership, you have little or no chance of negotiating a good price on a new car purchase.

The average American buys a new car every 6 years. Assuming this is accurate, there is no way you can compete with a salesperson who handles several contracts each day, and you, on the other hand, only make a purchase *once* every 2,190 days! It's impossible for you to beat them at "their own game." But, after you've read this book, you'll certainly have an advantage over 99% of the car-buying public.

This book will teach you how to be more aware of the environment you're dealing in, and give you knowledge to use to your advantage. It is designed to inform you of current automobile sales practices and how you can make the best possible deal.

Statistics say 9 out of 10 people spend an average of $500 or more per month for transportation. This is for one car payment, insurance, financing, repairs, gasoline and maintenance. Over a period of 48 months you probably have invested more than $24,000. Frightening, isn't it? With the price of luxury cars hitting over the $30,000 mark, that average investment is a considerable bit more.

When you look at the facts, you'll discover that most of you spend as much as 20% or more of your income on this vehicle payment. When you think of it this way, it is frightening! Certainly there must be a less expensive way and, there is.

The majority of car buyers take the words and advice of

a car salesperson as gospel. These charismatic individuals spend maybe 45 minutes with you to chart your transportation expense for the next 4 or 5 years! How do YOU know that THEY know what they're talking about? This salesperson may have been on the showroom floor for approximately 90 days—or 90 minutes—and might barely be qualified to explain the features and benefits of a toy truck much less an automobile.

They are not your friend. Although very few say they trust a car salesman and most hold them in such low esteem, yet most people blindly sign every paper placed in front of them and drive home in something new. Yes, the idea of driving home in a sparkling new vehicle to show your friends and family how successful you are causes you to make major mistakes.

As you're driving away, do you feel as though you've made the best deal possible? Do you feel that perhaps, you made a mistake? Do you have the new car owner's "buyers remorse"? Do you ever give a second thought as to how you're going to pay for this car or how much it will end up costing you?

I'm not going to tell you not to buy a new car because I think it's a thrill that everyone should experience at least once in their lifetime. It just feels good in that new car; the smell, the power of the engine, the easy shifting and it rides as if you were on a cloud, doesn't it?

Listen, I want you to have that new vehicle. I plan to help you save money by telling you what *they* do and how they do it, what *you* should do and how *you* should do it.

Contents

LET'S TALK

This book is divided into seven steps. Each will educate you about a facet of the automobile decision-making process. Some will apply to your particular situation, some will not. Throughout this book you will find useful worksheets to assist you in making the correct decisions when buying your next new car and selling the one you have.

Let's talk about why some people pay a whole lot for a car and others pay considerably less—and for the same car! That's an easy question to answer; the *uninformed* will always pay more. You, will not! Because why? Because I'll give you an inside look at the dealership so you can understand that the seven steps I've listed will save you thousands on your next new car purchase.

First, I want you to know that every dealership pays the *same price* for an identical vehicle. Whether the dealership is right next door to the automobile plant that manufactures the car or completely across the country from them, they pay *exactly the same!* It's the law of the franchise system.

So, how come one dealership sells a car for one price and

the other at a lower price? It all has to do with education. If you're an educated consumer you pay less. If you're uneducated, you pay more. And the less educated you are, the more you pay. That's why this book will help you. I'm going to make you among the most educated new car buyers in the world!

WHERE TO BUY

I would suggest that you buy your new vehicle at the location *nearest and most convenient* to where you live or work, mostly for service purposes. I've seen people drive several hundred miles "to get a deal" on a new car and they end up paying more for it than if they had bought it from a dealer around the corner.

Then, when something breaks, you have to either drive several hundred miles more to your selling dealer to get priority service, or you can take your new car to *any* dealership for service. But, trust the fact, you'll be the *last* to receive attention; the customers who bought the car from that particular dealership are, without question, given expedient service. Let me tell you more.

CUSTOMER SATISFACTION

Years ago, car dealerships felt that if they sold everybody in town one vehicle, it's all the money they ever needed. Whether they satisfied the customer or not didn't matter to them.

Nowadays, the focus is on pleasing, satisfying, actually spoiling the customer. It's termed "customer satisfaction." Owner loyalty is of utmost importance to the manufacturer, not because they truly care but because of the competition. It's no more, "Sell anybody anything and who cares what else happens" because manufactures predict that in the next six years, there will be more vehicles available than there are customers to buy them, due to the ever-expanding number of vehicle lines from which to choose.

German-made cars are more visible than ever; England has several fine cars; Korea seems to be introducing a new car brand every week; South America is building and selling cars; and our old nemesis, Japan is still kicking our butts. If manufacturers can't satisfy their customers today and build this customer loyalty, there won't be any buyers for their cars tomorrow. That's not to say they won't continue to try to make three, four or even five thousand dollars selling you a new car.

HOW DEALERSHIPS ORDER

Each dealership orders their stocking inventory from their respective manufacturers based on their sales patterns of the past. The types of cars they typically sell in a given region or area are ordered by the dealership. The assembly of cars is done at one particular plant, but the parts of these cars come from all over the world. For instance, Mexico makes manual transmissions for most manufacturers. Japan makes almost all the radios. Fuel injectors may be made in Switzerland and, car manufacturers don't make paint, they are bought from Dow or Dupont or wherever else they can get it at the right price. It's called "outsourcing".

Since manufacturers don't have the control they used to have when they made their own parts at their own plants, they often run out of popular items. This makes shortages of the more popular vehicles. The manufacturer must then allocate the new vehicles to their thousands of dealerships across the country. This is how they do it.

For instance, XYZ motor company has the availability to produce 50,000 Hutmobiles and they have 2,500 dealers. This doesn't necessarily mean that each dealer gets 20 each of these cars. Allocations are determined by individual sales history and *customer satisfaction index*!

There are mountains of forms to fill out and each outlines how their customers were treated. Some of these forms are filled out by salespeople, some by the dealership, and others are based on customer feedback. Remember that phrase, "Customer Satisfaction!" You can expect to be treated with more courtesy than ever before at your new car dealership because you, the customer, will keep these people in business.

Since cars cost all dealerships the same price, it is the convenience of the location, or the amount of success with advertising that will draw you to them. If they get you there, they had better sell you a car and in doing so, they have to be certain you are spoiled—satisfied. Remember, that's what they are after—the dealers and the manufacturers—customer satisfaction!

WHEN TO BUY A NEW CAR

One book I read said that the best time to go hunting for a car is in late fall or winter, when sales are slowest and deals are easiest to come by. Try shopping the last week of the month, when dealerships are competing in contests or pushing to meet sales quotas. If possible, shop late in the day at dinnertime or afterward—when salespeople and managers tend to be tired and more flexible about closing deals. There may be some truth to this.

But, I say . . . the best time to buy a new car is when YOU decide you want one! There is no best time. I know you think there is, but I'm telling you there isn't! Once you read all the information in this book, ANY time is the best time!

Many of you think you can wait until October to buy last year's model at a drastic discount, but you can't! A new car today will cost less to buy than that same new car tomorrow. A common misconception for many new car buyers is that last year's model has depreciated and that they can get it cheaper. Wrong! Because, on a quarterly basis, manufacturers increase their price to the dealers. Thus, the price of a new car increases with time, even one that's already had a birthday!

In other words, if you wait until October of 1996 to buy a 1995 model car, because of the quarterly increases in price by the manufacturer, you'll pay more for a one-year-old car than you would have had you bought it in October a year ago when it first arrived on the showroom floor! Conclusion: It is really not a good idea to buy a new, one-year-old car, the major reason being that in the unlikely event you have an accident and total the vehicle, or it's stolen, your insurance company will replace it at substantially *less* than what you paid because of the depreciation and the fact that it is considered a used vehicle.

Car ownership is the second largest expenditure you will ever make other than buying a home. At today's prices, you could probably spend almost as much on your car as you do on your home. So, let's begin by saving some money on the vehicle you have in your garage now.

Please, read this entire book. There's much to learn and

if you miss one significant point, it leaves you vulnerable to a salesperson's whim. Remember, these salespeople are good. They are trained until selling becomes an art with them. And they practice this art many, many times more than you so, without complete information, you'll pay more. Don't do that! I want this ten-dollar investment you made in this book to be one of the wisest expenditures you will ever make. Make me proud of you. Go out and get the best deal you can. Here's how.

Step 1

TURN YOUR OLD CAR INTO CASH

Usually the first thing an uneducated buyer/seller will do is to take their car to a dealership to trade it in on a new car. During the early stages of the negotiating process, they are asked for the keys. The salesman then drives the car off to some unknown place and returns—after what seems like an eternity—with a calculated grimace on his face and a piece of paper marked with a fat crayon from kindergarten:

ACV $2000

What's happened, is that the vehicle has just been appraised by the "Used Car Manager" whose primary function is to buy a car for as *little* as possible and to sell it for as *much* as possible.

Your heart will stop, your head begins to pound and you get that uneasy feeling. You *know* your car is worth more. The salesman notices your reaction and quickly begins to write on the pad. Ordinarily, you have no idea what the salesperson is talking about when he adds the *Discount & Rebate* to this number and now calls it your *Used Car Allowance*. This figure is more in line with what you wanted for your vehicle.

This is a scam; the rebate is what the manufacturer automatically puts on many new vehicles and will be deducted from the price anyway. Dealers use this as a way to bump the price of your trade-in vehicle and make it "look" as if you're getting more. Then, they'll throw in the $500 discount, which they also do anyway. Now, you are satisfied because it looks as if you're getting a super deal on your trade-in. You are not!

Remember, their object is to get a used car for as *little* as they can, and sell it for as *much* as they can. Which means, you get as little for your trade in as they can offer you without being condemned to hell forever. And they'll look you in the eye and tell you what you want to hear and all the time they have their hand in your pocket.

Most people take their car to three different dealerships and go through this process three times and then take the best offer. Some get so confused that they end up accepting the appraisal of the salesperson who seems the nicest, who they like the best. I want you to be able to negotiate like an expert.

YOUR FIRST MOVE

The first thing you need to do is evaluate your current position. Put your love and affection for your present car (truck, van, jeep, etc.) aside and deal with it academically, like the piece of merchandise that it is. Forget that it was the first car your second-to-last son was brought back from the hospital in, or that your teenager used it on his/her first driving test. It is a piece of machinery. Never fall in love with a "thing."

One of the most negotiable items in a vehicle transaction is your used car value. You can determine a realistic **ACV** (Actual Cash Value) on your own if you're equipped with the knowledge.

It's a toss-up as to which most people do first; either contact their banker and look at the Blue Book value of their car, or search the classified section of the newspaper to see what a similar car is selling for, or drive by used car lots and see what prices they have on cars *somewhat* like theirs; same make, year, model, options, mileage and general condition. One out of three ain't all bad!

What I'm saying is save your time. All you really need to do is look in a Used Car Guide Book that your banker who makes car loans undoubtedly has. It will give you the basics of what you need to know to determine the ACV (Actual Cash Value) of your present vehicle. Don't panic! We'll teach you to read this guide book later on in this chapter.

Assuming you now know *approximately* what your car is worth, let's go to the next step to get an even more accurate figure as to the *true* value of it.

EYE APPEAL

Eye appeal is very important. After all, it's probably the main reason that has led you to consider buying a new car. First, you liked the way it looked. The same is true with the car you are trying to sell or trade. It has to *appeal* to those who are in the market for buying a used car. This is what used car dealers look for.

✓What will your vehicle look like after it's reconditioned?

✓How will it "measure up" when parked next to others on the lot?

✓What percentage of the prospective buyers would consider your vehicle over other desirable ones?

Eye Appeal goes something like this. A **red** car is the most popular color. In a used car lineup they put a red car on each end. This causes people to look at the row. Red attracts attention.

I have a friend who has a 1990 Crown Victoria, white outside, blue interior. The car is a *jewel*. He bought it new, services it regularly by changing the oil and getting a new filter every 3000 miles, and the inside is immaculate. He doesn't smoke nor allow anyone to smoke in his car and he had it waxed every six months and the only repairs it ever needed was maybe getting new tires.

I have an acquaintance who has the exact car but it is a rose color, inside and out. He doesn't maintain it nearly as well, he is a chain smoker, and the car has 15,000 more miles than the one I mentioned above. Side by side on a used car lot, the rose-colored car would sell faster and for maybe $700 to $1,000 more than the white.

BECAUSE, most people look upon a white car as having belonged to an oil company or some service company where they drive it a lot. They are certain , regardless of what the odometer reads, that the car had 50,000 miles per year put on it. They just *know* that the 105,000 miles (where only the 5,000 mile reading shows), that it isn't 105,000 but 205,000; maybe even 305,000 miles.

When selling your present car to a dealer's lot and if it happens to be white, I'm not suggesting you paint it rose, just accept the fact that, from a used car manager's standpoint, it does not have the same eye appeal.

Eye appeal will either increase or decease the value of your car by $500 more than the guide book value. After considering all of the above, put what you feel is the value of the eye appeal of your car.

Assess the value of the eye appeal here: $ _____

RECONDITIONING COST

Before you can determine the true value of any vehicle, you need to find out how much it will cost you to recondition it. All guidebooks for used cars are for "showroom ready" vehicles. Let's see what it will cost to put yours in showroom condition.

✓Has it been hit more times than your horn?

✓Did someone turn an alligator loose in the front seat, or was it just your kids?

✓Does the transmission slip, or is it starting to?

✓Does the air conditioner or heater work properly? Are you getting just "dogs breath" out of your vents? Do you need more Freon, or maybe a new compressor?

✓Do the tires match, or are they badly worn?

✓Does it shimmy at 30, 40, or 60 miles per hour?

✓Does it need shocks? Brakes? A paint job?

✓Does it smell like you're trapped inside a cigarette butt?

For starters, do try to get the smoke smell out. Here's a tip on how to do it. Put 4 or 5 sheets of BOUNCE (scented sheets of paper that are used while drying clothes) under the seat and change them every two weeks. Within maybe 2 months, the smell is gone. Of course, don't continue to smoke in it, and throw away the ashtray and buy a new one!

Do not repair a vehicle that you are going to trade, unless it affects its ability to operate safely! Definitely, do not paint it, **clean it**! No need to put on new seat covers, or have the head liner repaired because dealerships can do it much cheaper. If your transmission slips or makes noise and you want a shock, take it to one of those fix-it places and get a price. Sometimes, the cost of a new or reconditioned transmission is half the value of the car, maybe even more than the entire car is worth.

If you have a clean vehicle, that is normally an indication of the overall condition and can add hundreds of dollars to the perceived value of it. Washing it only, is rarely sufficient. It costs on average from $50 to $100 for a complete detail and professional detailer's can work magic. You will almost always recover at least 2 to 4 times the cost you spend to have your vehicle detailed.

In selecting a detailer, look at the work they just did on

someone elses' vehicle. You want a detailer who won't get too "heavy at the wheel" and burn the paint off your car or swirl the finish too much.

Make a note of what is needed and an approximate minimal cost to repair the car properly. Your answers will affect the value of your vehicle. This is your workbook so circle the problems and estimate the cost of repairs here:

Your Assessment of Cost of Repairs: $ _____

> *Caution! Do not make costly repairs unless it effects the ability to operate the vehicle.*

BOOK VALUE

Now that your car has been detailed and looks really great, what does "the book" say the value of your vehicle is worth? Your next question should be *which* book? The N.A.D.A? The Black Book? The Kelly Blue Book? Or, the A.M.R. (just to list a few)?

The accepted standard book used across the country is the **N.A.D.A (National Automobile Dealers Association) Official Used Car Guide.** The *Kelly Blue Book* is simply a different brand of book that gives, basically, the same information as the N.A.D.A. guide. Over the years, the masses refer to the N.A.D.A. as the *Blue Book*, even though it is . . . yellow!

The *Black Book,* published weekly, is strictly auction reports and used mainly by wholesale buyers. The *A.M.R. (Auto Market Research)* mainly does research for the manufacturers.

A common comment in the used car business is that "the book never buys anything." No matter how much you try, you can't sell your car to a "book" for any price.

It isn't difficult to read any of these books but when visiting your banker, bring this book along with you and record the information you get from their N.A.D.A. book on the Book Value Worksheet.

The base number ordinarily used is the "Loan Value". Granted, this is the lowest value listed but we will build on this number to determine what the ACV (there's that Actual Cash Value again). If you use the letters ACV when dealing with a salesperson, this will get their attention and they will treat you with a bit more respect.

Remember, it's the bottom line. We want to, figuratively speaking, fold up that vehicle and put it in your wallet and the fatter the wallet, the better you've done your job.

Your banker or insurance agent will have a copy of the current N.A.D.A. Used Car Guide and it should take but a few minutes to get the numbers you need. I've created a worksheet for you. If you'll follow this guideline, you'll be that much farther ahead of the game. And if you do, in fact, treat this like a game, it will be fun and profitable.

Complete as much of the following information as possible while looking at your vehicle:

BOOK VALUE WORKSHEET

Options	Example	Your Car	Sample
Vehicle ID	17-digit# on windshield		*23D780L60013-4579E*
Make	Ford, Dodge, Mercedes, etc.		*Toyota*
Year			*1992*
Model	Tempo, F-150, GrandPrix, etc.		*Corolla*
Series	LX, or any other name on body		*DX*
Body Type	2dr, 4dr, Coupe		*4-Door*
Engine	V8, V6, 4Cyl., 350, 5.0 liter		*V-6*
Mileage	Odometer #		*59,026*

Look in the N.A.D.A. Guide and find the Average Loan Value of your vehicle. This figure is a base estimate which we will add or subtract the following:

Average Loan Value: $ _____

Look at the bottom of the page for possible directions to additional options to add or deduct. The N.A.D.A. book will have them listed such as, power windows. If you have them, you add. If you don't have air conditioning, you deduct, etc. I think the guide will be self-explanatory.

❏ Add or ❏ Deduct for:_____ $_____

❏ Add or ❏ Deduct for:_____ $_____

❏ Add or ❏ Deduct for:_____ $_____

❏ Add or ❏ Deduct for:_____ $_____

❏ Add or ❏ Deduct for:_____ $_____

❏ Add or ❏ Deduct for Mileage:_____ $_____

Total Average Loan Value including all additions and deductions equals N.A.D.A. Guide Loan or Book Value:

Your Assessment of Book Value: $ _____

Now, comes the shock of your life. Your vehicle in the N.A.D.A. Guide Book will list what to deduct for high mileage. I've seen a car valued to this point at over $5,000. Then, when the figure for the mileage was subtracted, it was worth $1,700. Frightening, I know. But, that's the way it is.

Of course you'd never sell your car for this amount. You'd rather keep it or give it away. That's your option. I'm only here to tell you the facts! Look at it this way. I know you're disappointed to find out that this vehicle is worth so little, but put the shoe on the other foot. If you were buying this car, would you pay $5,000 for it with 125,000 miles on the odometer?

So, at this point you will have a value for your vehicle as far as Eye Appeal, Reconditioning Cost, and Book Value. There is yet one more item, a *variable* that will determine the final value of your current vehicle.

CURRENT MARKET CONDITIONS

Who will give you, how much cash NOW for your vehicle? With the total of the first three considerations you've just read over (look back at them if you need to), you can determine if the amount you're offered is what you will accept.

The only constant in the automobile business is *change*! When the press released the rear-end collision problems with the *Pinto*, the value dropped like a hot rock. Sometimes there is a glut of used vehicles on the market. More often than not, nice used cars and trucks are in big demand because, the price of the new vehicles has risen astronomically and people *simply can't afford* a brand new vehicle, just a better, more current, used one.

Occasionally the value of used vehicles is considerably less, due to new car incentives, rental car fleet turnover, property tax time, the economy, area layoffs, the climate (if you're trying to sell a convertible), interest rates and a dozen other possible variables that may effect some areas.

Conversely, a big demand drives values up substantially overnight, at a time when everybody in the used car business simply runs out of good used cars or trucks at the same time. It happens that way. For instance, in Texas, go anywhere and try to buy a nice, two-year-old used Chevy Truck. There aren't any!

The actual *book value* on these cars isn't always accurate either, because of the diverse conditions aforementioned, and more than likely, the data is over three months old. Still, it's the closest we all have in estimating the value of it.

Take the total of the previous three values and now consider them to be the ACV of your current vehicle. This amount is what you should consider accepting from the first person who offers it.

The only way for you to determine the Current Market Conditions is to mark your vehicle up a couple of thousand dollars and try to sell it now! You can always come down.

Now is the time to retrieve your input and totals from the previous pages to arrive at the Actual Cash Value of your car. In other words, this total should be an acceptable amount for an offer. If you have a well-kept, solid, car that looks good, ask what you choose and get as much as you can, I'm just giving you facts.

Perhaps if the person buying your car hasn't read this book, you will get the price you'd like to get. If they have read it, you probably won't. You need not feel like the salesperson at the dealership if you get a high price for your fine car. They are programmed not to have feelings and many wouldn't give a deal to their own mother. You're not doing any wrong, just getting what you feel you deserve. They, the salespeople and the dealership, woefully, feel likewise.

You might subtotal the Eye Appeal, Reconditioning Cost, and Book Value. Look at this figure and try to determine how much *more* somebody else would pay for your vehicle. And enter your guesstimate of current market conditions. This total is the ACV "Actual Cash Value".

Eye Appeal:	$
- Reconditioning Cost:	$
+ Book Value:	$
= Subtotal:	$
+ Current Market Conditions:	$
= ACV Actual Cash Value:	$

SALES TAX

In many states you are given credit for the sales tax on the value of your trade-in. When you trade or purchase another vehicle, in Texas for example, the sales tax on a car is (currently) 6.25% of the trading difference between the purchased vehicle and the traded vehicle.

To maximize your cash position, you should add this tax savings to your asking price for your used vehicle if you don't trade it in on a new car.

Let's say your current vehicle has, for example (in Texas), an ACV of $10,000. Add 6.25% or $625 (State Sales Tax) to the ACV to get the minimum acceptable price of $10,625.

	Your Vehicle	Sample
+ Actual Cash Value:		$10,000
+ Tax Savings:		$ 625
= Minimum Selling Price:		$10,625

Step 2

SELL YOUR CURRENT VEHICLE

I tried to make this book as easy as possible to read and to follow. Don't be hesitant to mark on these charts, they guide you step by step. If you want, use a pencil and for your next new car purchase, erase what you wrote for this one. Better yet, buy another book. Yeah, I like that idea . But please, follow this system and use these charts.

Now that you know what you plan to ask for your car, you need to learn how to sell it. A close friend of mine, who happens to be one of the best automobile salesmen I've ever known, once had a sign posted is his office that read:

Hoss trading is alright,
so long as the other feller has the best hoss.

There are only two markets in which to sell your current vehicle if you choose not to trade it on a new one; RETAIL and WHOLESALE. Let's start off with the retail market.

RETAIL MARKET

The Retail market is the most difficult, and therefore, should net you the most cash. If you choose the newspaper route, other than having to answer the telephone at all hours, be prepared to contend with strangers in your home. In pricing your car you have a few choices; either list it for a realistic figure according to what you've determined you can get for it or list it for maybe $1,000 more because people will offer you less or ask if this is the lowest price you'll accept. I say bump the price at least $1,000 maybe $1,500.

The fact is, the buyer might reason you've bumped the price and if you take less, they are pleased. Whereas, if you don't bump the price, most people figure you've bumped it anyway and therefore, you can't offer them a "deal" and you'll either not sell your car, take longer to sell it, or maybe not get the price you really want. Silly stuff, I know, but having dealt with the buying and selling public for over 20 years, that's the way it is.

So, if you have a car that you determine is worth $10,000, I recommend that you ask $11,000 for it (or $11,500) to reach that bump. If you plan to add your 6.25% tax you'll have to pay when buying your new car, that asking figure jumps up at least an additional $625 (6.25% sales tax times $10,000). Are you following me? That brings your *asking price* up to $11,625.

SELL TO FAMILY OR FRIENDS

By far, the easiest retail market to tap are those in your "circle of influence", i.e. your friends, relatives, neighbors, and co-workers. There is always a problem because friends or relatives want either a special price or maybe to pay some now and some later. If you sell to a friend or relative, you'll have to think about dealing with repair problems *after* the sale not counting the ill-will you'll create. I say sell to a stranger! If you do decide to try friends or relatives, these are my suggestions:

✓Get cash! No credit and no terms and don't hold the car for them to gather the money.

✓Deal straight with them—to a point. I don't see a problem in telling them that you already have a few people interested in the car. This will usually spur them into making a decision quickly.

✓Tell them you plan to sell your car to the first person with cash and that you will have the vehicle sold within the week. It should not take longer than two weeks to sell.

✓It's both smart and honest to tell them what is good and what the defects are in the car to avoid future implications. Even vehicles in good condition often break down with major, expensive problems.

	Your Vehicle	Sample
Minimum Selling Price:		$10,625
+ Compensation:		$ 1,000
= Retail Selling Price:		$11,625

Consider carefully any offer in excess of the Minimum Selling Price. Remember, only *you* will know your "comfort zone" when it comes to the amount of cash you get for your vehicle. You know what it's worth because you got the N.A.D.A. book value, you know how well you've cared for it, how dependable it's been, how comfortable it is to drive, and you've been realistic with yourself on appraising it.

Experience has taught me that the *first reasonable cash offer* for your current vehicle is as much or more than any other offer you'll get! And it usually ceases to exist once turned down. I'm not proposing you abandon your good Poker face, really convincing gestures, controlled body language, and a few, "Well's...", and " I don't know's..." but, sell to the first reasonable offer!

You Can Do Much More With The Cash Than The Car!

WHOLESALE MARKET

If you don't want to hassle with the Retail Market there is another avenue you can take, the Wholesale Market. You can get a lot of money for your car, very quickly, from the Wholesale Market! While the *amount* of money you get will probably not be as much as if you retailed your car, you can get much more money for it than you would have if you traded it in to a dealer.

> *You can sell your car, for cash, directly to a Used Car Retailer. They buy used cars for their lots at wholesale prices.*

There are wholesalers who buy used cars from dealers, individuals, and auctions, then sell them to other dealers. They buy a car from one lot that can't market it, and sell it to another lot that has a clientele for that type of vehicle. They are usually retired used car managers that saved enough money to pay cash for a car or two. They go from lot to lot, buying one car at a lot and driving it to another lot and selling it. They then buy a different car from that lot and drive it to another lot and repeat the process again. If they make a bad decision, they take it to an auction, bail out and start over.

They have winners and losers, but for a good wholesaler, most are winners. A wholesaler usually makes from $500 to $1,000 per car doing this. When you trade your vehicle in, the dealer will hold this much from your allowance in case he has to wholesale your vehicle. You can eliminate this "middle man" and pocket this money yourself!!

Which Used Car Lot do you take it to? I'll tell you. But first, you'll have to classify your vehicle. A retail Used Car Dealer looks at a vehicle and classifies it as either a **Retail Piece** or a **Wholesale Piece**.

A Retail Piece is a car that is usually on the higher end of the used car price scale; the type car they think they can sell on their lot at retail quickly, at a profit. It will probably need very little reconditioning.

A Wholesale Piece is a car that is usually on the *lower* end of the used car price scale. It could be an older car or even a newer one that's been "rode hard and put up wet." It could be that it just has a few hundred thousand miles on it. If your car needs a lot of reconditioning to make it "Front Line" ready, it's probably a Wholesale Piece.

Evaluate your current vehicle whether you believe it is wholesale or retail quality: _____

WHERE TO SELL A RETAIL PIECE

If you want to wholesale your retail piece, you should take it to a New Car Dealership's Used Car Lot. **This should be a lot that sells the same make that you have.** They have a natural market for your vehicle.

New car dealers buy used cars for their lots from wholesalers, auctions and any source they can. There are rarely enough quality trade-ins to supply their used car operation. You will usually get the most money from them. You simply drive to the used car lot and ask for the Used Car Manager. You might inform the salesman who greets you that you are not in the market to buy a car, you are there to sell one.

Add the "Wholesaler's" average profit (compensation) to your Minimum Selling Price.

	Your Vehicle	Sample
Minimum Selling Price		$10,625
+ Compensation		$ 500
= Wholesale Sales Price		$11,125

Don't be too quick to come off your price. Remember he wants to buy for as little as possible. Stick to your guns, tell him that you will take it to another lot if he doesn't buy at your figure. You can always return and sell it to him at his offer as a last resort.

WHERE TO SELL A WHOLESALE PIECE

If you find that your retail piece is really a wholesale piece, all is not lost. There are numerous used car lots that don't belong to New Car Dealers who are usually more diverse in the quality of their cars and who will take the time to do more reconditioning. They pay a decent price for a used car that needs a little work done or has more than a few miles on it.

Look for the ones with the more expensive used cars on their lots. They don't get as many nice trade-ins and have to buy cars from the wholesalers. You might be able to get your price from them fairly easily. It doesn't hurt to try.

If your vehicle is *rough*, but it's not quite time for the crusher, there is still a market left. We have a saying in the car business, "There's an ass for every seat!"

A Note Lot takes your old car, paints $500 on the windshield and writes the word "DOWN" after it. Then, some unfortunate person on the lower end of the buying public pays the $500 down, (which is usually the entire price the Note Lot paid for the car), and $25 a week until they can't pay anymore. The note lot repossesses the car and starts the cycle all over again until it's ready for the crusher or sold to a junk yard for parts.

If your car is in this problem category, and you have guts enough to drive to the dealership looking for a trade, the used car manager at the new car dealership will accurately disclose the ACV to you more so than if you drove in a decent car due to the low value of the car and the difficulty in disposing of these type vehicles. You can either accept or reject that figure.

My suggestion is, if you have a junker or near-junker, **don't make any repairs** and if you want to maximize your cash position, *you* take your vehicle to the Note Lots. You'll be surprised at how much more you will get for your old clunker.

These note lots can be anywhere, usually scattered along business areas of lower income neighborhoods. You've noticed them before but paid little mind since it had nothing to do with you —then! You remember the places now, don't you? The signs on these car lots that read, "We Buy Used Cars", or "We Buy, Sell and Trade Cars."

Just drive your car in and somebody will come out of the little hut, shack or trailer and come up to your car. Tell them you are planning on getting a new car and want a "Bid to Buy." These guys know cars better than anyone because it's probably their lot and they know what they can sell your car for. There are always folks with horrible credit who will pay outrageous prices for junk as long as it runs.

They will ask to drive it, come back after taking it for a

spin around the block, look around it, open the hood, check the engine, open the trunk, look at the condition of the interior and upholstery, and in minutes, give you a price.

Some might not even take it off their lot, just get in, start it, back it up, then look it over. By doing this, experienced used car lot owners can determine if your brakes are bad or the transmission slips. They can correct a lot of these problems with a simple wheel alignment or balancing the tires, perhaps replacing a tire or two. You should now have sold your car.

If, however, you have an outstanding balance on your car, it is much simpler if you sell to a reputable new or used car dealer. First you need to know the exact payoff from the lending institution that holds the title. Call them on the telephone, give them your account number and ask for an exact payoff that is good for at least ten days.

If you have the cash to pay it off, go to the lending institution and trade the cash for your title. *Be certain to get the title as you pay it off!* My experience has been that many banks and lending institutions will take your cash payoff then want to *send you* the title. Don't let that happen! Ask for the title right away and don't leave that place without it. They have it there. A lazy clerk might not want to look it up and sign the papers but they have it. Where else would they keep it?

VEHICLE EQUITY

Complete the following formula:

	Your Vehicle	Sample
Wholesale Selling Price:		$11,125
– Outstanding Balance:		$ 2,000
= Vehicle Equity:		$ 9,125

The dealer buying your car will verify the payoff and vehicle identification number with the lending institution and give you a check for your equity. An outstanding balance is an inconvenience but not a major problem. If you are selling to an individual, have your buyer go with you to your lending institution with the cash. Pay off the vehicle and transfer the title during the same trip. Should you need a notary, there is usually one available.

You will have, by now, "Turned Your Car Into Cash." More than likely, much *more* cash than you would have received had you tried to trade it in on a new car.

Remember part of the "inner workings" of a dealership is that they add the factory rebates and discounts to your trade-in value to mask the true allowance for your vehicle.

RENT-A-CAR

Now that you've sold your vehicle (assuming you don't have a second car or a friend you'll inconvenience into riding you around until you get another car), how will you get from point A to point B without a vehicle? You probably have some idea as to what kind of vehicle you would like to buy, so *rent one* like it for a couple of days. In fact, it's smart to rent one anyway. It's worth the hundred or so dollars for a three-day rental that will make you positive that this is, in fact, the vehicle you want to own.

Step 3

COUNT YOUR CASH

The one thing I find that amazes people the most, is how little they need to put down on a vehicle purchase if their credit rating is good or even just fair. Many lending institutions will finance the entire transaction without any down payment at all. A good credit rating also opens the door to extended term financing and low interest rates.

If, however, you have stumbled in the past or even fallen flat on your face, all is not lost. Lending institutions that used to almost throw somebody out the front door for having been 30 days late are taking a closer look at the customers they were missing.

There are many lending institutions out there that don't charge any application fees to give you the terms and conditions of a secured loan on an automobile. The auto manufacturer's credit companies are often the most lenient. They know they have a greater risk on customers with less-than-perfect credit ratings and compensate for this exposure by requiring additional down payments, shorter terms, by charging a slightly higher interest rate and by asking more information. Hey, it's business! You made a mistake or had bad luck and you have to pay for it.

In today's climate, a raised rate is less than yesterday's rates for the best customers. I think that, unless you're Jesse James, you can get a good auto-loan now.

CREDIT

You need to consider your other obligations before you sign up for a major monthly expense. The lender will look at your *debt-to-income ratio* to determine your "probability of payment" which affects the rate you will qualify for. Gather all of your bills and check out your interest rates on your outstanding consumer debts.

I'm giving you a worksheet for this too, and although it doesn't seem to have anything to do with buying a new car, it does! This sheet will assist you with your calculations and help you eliminate many or all of those bills, especially those 18%'ers and 21%'ers.

PERCENTAGE RATES

You see, what inexperienced people never think of, is the *percentage rate* charged by many credit card companies and department stores. After careful examination, you'll find that many department store credit cards are at 21%, most gasoline cards are a minimum of 18%, and jewelry stores are right up there at 18-21%. The payments are usually so low that most people don't realize what they are paying in interest.

If you total those bills, you will find a terrific monthly savings by paying their entire balance. Let me give you an example of how you can do it with your new car purchase.

Your car can put even more cash in your pocket!

This is the plan. Take the money that you just got for selling your car and put it to one side. I'm now going to show you how to save even more cash by *eliminating* those high interest loans with your vehicle equity.

Gather all your bills and list them on the Consumer Debt Worksheet that follows this explanation. By doing this, you will be able to see the high interest you are paying on these debts and pay them off with this money I asked you to push over to the side, the money you just got by selling your car.

In doing this, your monthly cash outlay will be less therefore accomplishing several things. The first, your *Debt to Income Ratio* will be improved. Second, you will not be "throwing money away" by paying high interest, because third, your new car loan will, without question, be at a lower interest rate than these other accounts. And lastly, you will (if you choose) be able to buy a nicer new car with this money you've saved from those high-interest accounts.

Consumer Debt Worksheet

Account Name	Total Balance Owed	Total Monthly Payment	%Rate	Monthly Savings if Paid	Interest Amount Paid	Interest Savings if Paid
Totals						

GROSS MONTHLY INCOME

To determine the maximum monthly payment that you can comfortably afford for a new vehicle is the principle key in starting on the right foot to getting a good deal.

Most lending institutions will usually decline a low-down-payment-vehicle-application if the monthly payment on the loan is greater than 20% of the applicant's gross monthly income. Many people, in the rush and confusion of buying an automobile, either don't know or can't recall their gross monthly income.

The most common mistake is to put their "take home pay" on the application. This almost always results in conditions from the lender such as additional down payment, reduced amount financed, or a flat turn-down of the loan.

> *Your gross monthly income is how much money you earn before deductions of any kind. This includes overtime pay and any other income that you earn.*

Assuming you've worked at one place for a year or more, get a copy of your income tax form, look at the figure marked "total income" and divide by 12. That is your **Gross Monthly Income.** Easy enough, huh?

If you've worked a job less than a year, say for six or so months, take your most *recent* month-ending paycheck stub and find your "Year To Date Gross" (YTD). It should be the largest number on your stub. Divide the Year To Date Gross by the number of months that you've worked, and get that figure.

If your income varies, or you have a second or part-time job, that raises your income. The lender wants to know what your Gross Income is per month so they can add what you are buying and paying and how much is left over. You are going to want your Gross Monthly Income to be as high as truthfully possible to assist in obtaining low or no down payment financing at the lowest possible interest rate.

If you are using your monthly check stubs, pull and copy your most recent four. Lenders often ask for these to verify this number. They usually call this "proof of income". If you don't have them, they will ask for W-2 Income Tax copies and other personal documents.

Remember, the Total Gross Income is income earned by *you and your spouse* and any extra pay either of you might earn. Add these two incomes to determine your afford ability.

Formula For Maximum Car Note:	Your Car	Sample
Your Gross monthly Income:		$ 2,000
+ Spouse's GMI:		$ 1,500
= Total Gross Monthly Income:		$ 3,500
x Multiply by 20% (.20):		$ 700
= Max. Affordable Vehicle Payment:		$ 700

This is the most money the lending institution will usually let you have. This may or may not be your maximum affordable vehicle payment; it probably will not be. I'll go into greater detail on this subject in Step 6, the chapter on FINANCING.

CONVERT PAYMENTS TO DOLLARS

In counting your money, at some point in time, you are going to need to convert payments to dollars. I don't know how many times I've heard from vehicle prospects that they don't care how much a vehicle costs, as long as their payments are low enough where they can pay for it.

Most people can't relate to cash. Whether a vehicle is $10,000 or $20,000 or $50,000 makes no difference. It's the monthly payments they'll understand. If I had a new Cadillac to sell for either $10,000 cash or $299 a month forever, I'd sell 1,000 to 1 with payments.

Also, if I asked you how high $20,000 in a stack of twenty-dollar bills is, you probably couldn't tell me, but almost everybody can relate to $400 a month. Converting payments to dollars and vice versa—exactly—usually requires a computer.

The payment is never posted on the window sticker of a new car; the *MSRP (Manufacturer's Suggested Retail Price)* is. By using the Factor Chart, you can get the price on a car window and find out how much your monthly payments will be. You can get within a dollar or two by using the Factor Chart to get your factor and these payment formulas.

PAYMENT FORMULAS

→Payment Formula 1: When you know what the payment is, and want to calculate the amount financed.

Example: (Payment) ÷ (factor) = Amount Financed
             $300 per month for 60 months @ 12% APR
             ($300) ÷ (.022244) = $13,486.78

→Payment Formula 2: When you know the amount financed and want to know what the payment is.

Example: (Amount Financed) x (Factor) = Payment
             $10,000 financed for 60 months @ 9% APR
             ($10,000) x (.020758) = $207.58 per month

Payment Factor Chart

			Term In Months			
%	24	36	42	48	52	60
5	.043871	.029971	.026003	.023029	.018871	.018871
6	.044321	.030422	.026456	.023485	.021887	.019333
7	.044773	.030877	.026914	.023946	.02235	.019801
8	.045227	.031336	.027377	.024413	.02282	.020276
9	.045685	.0318	.027845	.024885	.023295	.020758
10	.046195	.032267	.028317	.025363	.023776	.021247
11	.046608	.032739	.028794	.025846	.024263	.021742
12	.047073	.033214	.029276	.026334	.024756	.022244
13	.047542	.033694	.029762	.026827	.025255	.022753

You are now ready to finish counting your cash. Determine how much you can spend on a new vehicle without going broke trying to make the payments.

Add the "Vehicle Equity" to the "Maximum Affordable Finance Amount". This sum plus any additional down payment is ordinarily what most spend on an automobile purchase. A car salesperson will usually probe until they determine this amount.

They will try to sell you the least expensive automobile they can get you to take, for this amount. You will only become aware of this amount when you are in the finance office signing the contracts to take your new vehicle home. You are driving down the street grinning from ear-to-ear with a new car, broke but happy.

The dealer is now taking 20% of your income for the next five years, plus your savings, and the cash he gets from your trade-in to the bank so that he can buy another dealership to add to the 27 dealerships he already has.

> *With a little planning, you can get the new vehicle you want and save hundreds of dollars, probably thousands.*

In the best of circumstances, the amount financed is all you would like to spend on a new vehicle, call it "Ideal Vehicle Expenditure". You could keep your Vehicle Equity, either reduce or eliminate your Consumer Debt, and have more "fun money" to spend on something else. You have also saved by not having to come up with a down payment, and if you consolidated those high-interest charge cards, you will realize even more savings from not having as many bills to pay each month.

Your Ideal Vehicle Expenditure: $ _____

Since Mr. Murphy usually intercedes with his law, let's do a little more counting and compiling to produce another number that will be a little more typical. Hopefully, it will be closer to what it will take to fulfill your transportation desires without sending you to the poor house.

Vehicle Equity:	$
(minus) Amount Spent On Consumer Debt:	$
(equals) **Available Cash:**	$

Maximum Affordable Vehicle Payment:	$
(minus) Any Other Existing Vehicle Payments:	$
(minus) Any Increased Auto Insurance Payment:	$
(equals) **Total Available Vehicle Payment**:	$

Assume 60 Months @ an % rate of what is available:	$
(divide) Total Available Vehicle Payment by Factor:	$
(equals) Total Available Cash From Financing:	$
(plus) Available Cash for Down Payment:	$
(equals) **Total Vehicle Expenditure**:	$

PLANNING FOR THE BIG SURPRISE

The Total Vehicle Expenditure is not what you have to spend on a vehicle itself; this number includes:

- ✗ All applicable taxes
- ✗ Title fees
- ✗ License fees
- ✗ Documentary fees
- ✗ Extended Service policy
- ✗ Credit life insurance
- ✗ Accident & health insurance
- ✗ Alarm systems
- ✗ Rust proofing
- ✗ Paint sealers
- ✗ Fabric protectors

✗ Mobile telephone
✗ Window etching
✗ Window tint
✗ Audio systems
✗ Specialty tires and wheels
✗ Etc.

▶ All Applicable taxes—The exact amounts of these items are difficult to calculate everywhere because state laws vary. For generalization purposes, let's assume you are in Texas. Texas allows the charging of a fee for the Vehicle Inventory Tax which is .00023 times the Selling Price of the vehicle. The State Sales Tax is 6.25% of the Selling Price minus the Trade-In Allowance. You should have no trade-in at this juncture.

▶ Fees—The Documentary Fee is regulated in Texas at no more than $50. Since license and title fees vary by vehicle and county, we will use $100 as a average amount.

▶ Extended Service Policy—If you plan keep a vehicle a number of years (not wise) or if you drive a lot of miles, an extended service policy is often a good buy. The vehicle manufacturer generally offers the best service policy at a cost of from $1,000 to $1,500. However, most vehicles come with a minimum of 36 months, or 36,000 miles, bumper-to-bumper factory warranty. Some new cars have a 5-year, 50,000 mile warranty.

If you want an extended service policy, let me tell you the best type to buy. If I were buying a Ford, I'd want a policy with the Ford name on it. If I were buying a Chevrolet, I'd want the GM name on it. If I were buying a Chrysler, well, you get the idea. These manufacturer's service policies are the best because they won't go out of business. You have no out-of-pocket expense except your deductible while getting the covered service work performed, and a lot less hassle.

"In-house" or other brand service policies are often unacceptable as payment at many service shops. You may have to pay for your repair, file a claim, and hopefully they will reimburse you.

▶ Insurance—Credit Life is term life insurance offered when you sign a retail installment contract. Accident and Health Insurance (sometimes called disability insurance) is a policy that in the event you are sick or disabled and unable to work, pays your car installment. My advice: Pass on the Life & Health insurance, see your insurance agent for a better deal.

Credit Life Insurance and Accident & Health Insurance varies in price according to the amount financed. For estimation purposes, use $500 for each person covered by "Credit Life" and use $1,500 for "Disability" or "Accident & Health Insurance".

▶ Alarm Systems—There are alarm systems and there are more alarm systems. The most common are Remote Actuated which include a shock sensor and a voltage sensor that trips the alarm when a door is opened, hood is raised, or anything that might cause a light to turn on inside the vehicle. Most trunks have a light so the voltage sensor will actuate. The remote operations are normally with a key pad that you put on your key chain. Normally, they will either lock or unlock your doors from approximately 50 feet or unlock the trunk. There are the silent kind as well as those that make a sort of "turkey" call. Theft deterrent systems are often good ideas in these days and times and will cost between $500 to $1,000 for a good one with remote operation.

▶ Rust Proofing—Most manufacturers guarantee their vehicles against "perforation" rust (all the way through, not surface rust) for five years or 100,000 miles. Some rust proofing vendors offer a lifetime guarantee (still not for surface rust). Additional protection is recommended if your vehicle is regularly exposed to salt or other corrosive elements.

▶ Paint Sealers—Essentially it's a silicone based process that fills the pores of the paint and reduces or eliminates oxidation of the paint. I know you expect the manufacturer will already have done this, but the paint needs time to cure and manufacturers turn cars out and ship them as fast as they can. Therefore to insure your paint job, this additional paint sealer should be put on your vehicle about the time it reaches the dealer. If you get this paint sealer when you buy the vehicle, the dealer will save you time and effort by putting it on then. I say pass on the paint sealer.

▶ Fabric Protectors—Again, manufacturers often *Scotch Guard* the fabric on seats of new cars. Fabric protectors are now usually included in with the rust proofing and paint sealer so it doesn't cost anything. If your vehicle is not Scotch Guarded, you can get the dealer to do it for you. The truth of the matter is, you can go to your local supermarket, and buy a can of Scotch Guard and do it yourself for less than ten bucks. If you have leather seats, the best thing to use is a quality leather cream. I like Haverty's.

Rust, Paint, and Fabric Protection when properly applied, has it's merits and will usually cost $500.

▶ Window Etching—A process by which they install your serial number on the vehicle's windows by use of a hydrofluoric acid and a stencil. This is an aid in identifying your vehicle after it's been stolen. Most manufacturers label every other structural piece of your vehicle. My suggestion: It's overkill. Pass the etching.

▶ Window Tint—An extraordinary way to extend the life of the interior of your vehicle by keeping the ultraviolet rays of the sun off your fabrics. It is also somewhat of a coolant and reduces the temperature inside the vehicle substantially. Before you get total black tint, consult the state laws. For instance, you cannot have it totally blacked out. There is a margin on the top of your windshield called "the Eyebrow". It is from six to eight inches wide and does an excellent job at keeping the sun from blinding you in the late afternoon.

▶ Audio Systems—Most cars now come with a quality audio system. But, to satisfy the *audiophile,* the system can be upgraded. Audio disc changers are growing in popularity meteorically. The 10-disc units work well with the AM/FM radios (which include the cassette player). If you really care about the music, take it to a radio shop and get exactly what you want. They will give you custom work and usually charge you less.

I am often asked the question about option packages. Women ask if they are required to buy a "package" that includes a lighted make-up mirror as well a some other "stuff" they don't want.

This is what has happened. Through countless surveys, the auto manufacturers have learned what the most common packages requested are. It is not price-effective for them to have 60 separate options on each vehicle. By offering packages, they can reduce the cost. With this limited variation in options, the assembly line can make fewer mistakes and get these cars out more quickly to the consumer.

Take the extra stuff and learn to live with it is my suggestion. The fact is that if you order power windows, they usually just "throw in" power locks and vanity (lighted visor mirrors).

I guess it's impossible to get exactly what you want without having to take a few things you don't want. Hey! I'm on your side. I'm only writing this book and telling you about it, I'm not manufacturing these cars.

Let's take, for example, that you want to buy a car at Dealer Cost and the price is exactly $25,000:

1. Taxes—State sales tax (Texas) 6.25% and VIT [Vehicle Inventory Tax] is: .23% or 6.48% x $25,000 = $1,620
2. Title fees $25
3. License fees (and Inspection) $75
4. Documentary fees $50
5. Extended service policy $1500
6. Credit life insurance $400

7. Accident & health insurance $1500
8. Alarm systems $600
9. Rust proofing $300
10. Paint sealers $150
11. Fabric protectors $100
12. Mobile telephone $300
13. Window etching $100
14. Window tint $175
15. Audio systems $600
16. Specialty tires and wheels $700
17. Etc. . . . . ???

These "extras" total over $8,100. Add this to the $25,000 and it comes out to be $33,100. If you plan to finance that for 5 years at 10% APR, it comes out to be only $703 per month. But, that $25,000 vehicle you just love, will end up costing you $42,180 plus gasoline, plus maintenance plus insurance.

I can't determine how much gasoline you'll use, since I don't know how far you drive. I can't help with the amount of your insurance because, I'm not privy to your driving record. Just for grins, let's estimate a few things. Let's say you drive but 20,000 miles a year and you get 20 miles per gallon. In five years you have used about $6,500 in gas.

If you have an oil and filter change every 3,000 miles, add about $665 to that. And, assuming you have a flawless driving record, you're over 25 years of age and you need complete coverage since your car is being financed, you can (safely) tack on an additional $1,500 a year or another $7,500. Forget about washing and waxing and minor repairs but your tires won't last but 30,000 miles and at a cost of about $450 per change, that's another $1,500.

Do you want that total? Can you take it? It comes out to be . . . $58,345 for five years of driving. Oh, you like time payments. It only comes out to be $31.97 . . . a day! You can afford that! No problem, right?

Yes, it is frightening when you think about it, isn't it? And, you are one of the fortunate to have read this book and you made the **absolute best deal possible!** Think of the ones who aren't as informed as you.

What this "dose of reality" does to you is to better equip you to purchase the vehicle you can, now, safely afford.

Total Vehicle Expenditure (from Previous Chart):	$
(minus) Optional Credit Life Insurance:	$
(minus) Optional Disability Insurance:	$
(minus) Optional Extended Service Policy:	$
(minus) Documentary Fee:	$
(minus) License and Title Fees:	$
(equals) **Sub Total for Tax Calculations:**	$
(divided by in Texas) 1.0648 (1+Sales Tax Rate of .0625+Inventory Tax of .00023):	$
(equals) **Total Price Vehicle+Taxable Options:**	$
(minus) Optional Theft Deterrent System Cost:	$
(minus) Optional Rust, Paint, Fabric Protection:	$
(minus) Another Optional After-Market Accessory:	$
(minus) Another Optional After-Market Accessory:	$
(equals) **Maximum To Spend on a Vehicle:**	$

This is the amount of money that you have calculated to be the maximum amount you should spend for buying a new vehicle. Now that you know what you *should* spend, you can decide what to actually spend it on and the car you can afford. At last count there were 58 different brands of vehicles from which to choose.

Step 4

SELECT A NEW VEHICLE

In today's market, there is no wonder most people dislike dealing with a car salesperson. Their job is to help you select the vehicle you want, from his present inventory, on the first day that you visit the dealership. They know that, if this is not accomplished, another car salesperson or dealership will ultimately get your business. You are there, specifically, because you want to buy a new car.

The salespersons are paid by commission and will get nothing for their efforts if you don't buy. Most customers are aware of this, but don't know what to do about it. Thus, the feeling of predator and prey prevails. You run and they chase. Contrary to popular belief, most car salesmen have retractable fangs. And, your knowledge of how the process works will enable you to feel more comfortable. You'll get the exact vehicle you want, at the best price possible.

SOME TRICKS OF THE TRADE

These salespeople are, for the most part, fairly nice individuals. Most of them endure 12 to 14 hour days, 6 days a week just to get the opportunity to be of service to you, and, of course, to make a commission that they will gladly earn.

As a rule, believe it or not, automobile dealerships and sales personnel are honest, trustworthy and honorable. Whether they are honest and honorable, etc., may not be their choice; they are governed by a State Regulatory Commission that protect the consumer's rights and interests. But like your car, some are a little more polished than others.

You drive your car into a new car dealership and walk through the large glass doors leading to the sales floor. If they're on their toes, a sales person will greet you with a wide smile, handshake, and introduce themselves.

My editor asked if sometimes you walk in and begin to look at the cars on the display floor and when you seem to be paying particular attention to a certain vehicle, then the salesman will approach and ask if they can be of help.

Rarely if ever. These salesman are always in the "attack mode" and should not let you wander aimlessly about. They are trained to be there when you need them.

You might wonder why many do not offer you their business card at the beginning. It's because, when you are through looking, and ask for the business card, they will usually slap their pockets signifying that they don't have one, then ask you to follow them into their office. Here, they will find their business card in their desk and at the same time, have a pad and pencil ready to get information on you; your name, address, telephone numbers, etc.

The primary objective of a car salesperson is to:

✓Sell you a vehicle that cost as little as possible.

✓Sell you one from the current inventory.

✓Sell it for as much as possible.

✓Sell it as quickly as possible.

Invariably, the successful car salesperson must attempt to reach into your pocket and count the money in your wallet. To do this, they ask you a series of questions:

1. "How much do you want to spend on your new car?" Nice, polite, understandable question, isn't it? There are a few key words in that simple, understandable question; the first is "want to spend" and the second, on *your* new car. They want to instill in you from the start, this is going to be *your* new car. Selling is beautiful, isn't it?

2. "How much to you have to put down?" You'll then tell them you have a car to trade or if you've sold it, how much cash you'd "like" to put down. And, in the same breath, the big question is . . .

3. "How much do you want your monthly payments to be?" Now this is where you'll have to read the section about financing because it used to be that a new car would be sold on a 36-month plan. Then a 48-month plan and now, it isn't

uncommon for a 60-month plan (even a 72-month plan)! Do you see, the dealerships and manufacturers want to make that monthly payment as low as they can so that you can, in fact, be able to afford almost any car in the world.

4. Now they ask, "What kind of trade-in do you have?" If you have a trade in, the next question is . . .

5. "Do you have a balance on your vehicle?" This next question is what we call "implied consent" as the sales-person rises, smiles and points his arm towards the show room floor and asks . . .

6. "What price vehicle do you want to see first?"

Is this a class act, or what? If it's done correctly, a good salesperson will let the words flow, write down the figures, and move about with the grace and charm of a choreo-graphed dancer.

All the questions are reasonable. You're there asking about a certain vehicle and your answers enables the salesman to save your time and theirs because they need to know the approximate price range and type of vehicle to show you.

You will, usually if not willingly, answer all of these questions. With a wry smile when asked how much you want to spend, most people say, "As little as possible." Thus begins the struggle between buyer and seller. This struggle is often called "negotiating". The typical salesperson practices this art form four or five times a day, six days a week. You, on the other hand, only practice automobile negotiating, on an average of once every six years.

Salesman: "Good evening!"

Buyer A: Smiles, says good evening then sits down at the salesman's desk. The next thing she says is, "Look, I'm going to be candid. I hate high-pressure sales tactics. I am asking for your best price and if it's good, I'll buy the car tonight, and if it isn't, I'll walk and you'll never see me again."
  Do you know the only words that salesman heard? "I'll buy the car tonight." When Buyer A told him she didn't want to be high-pressured, she gave the salesman all the information he needed to make the sale. Of course, he would never high-pressure her. He was already counting his commission.

  A friend who was a siding salesman told me this story. He hadn't made a siding sale in a week. The lady he was talking to (pitching) said she was a widow and after his presentation, she excused herself and went out of sight for maybe five minutes. The salesman patiently waited. "I can't take the deal," the lady said when she returned. "My husband said it was a bad deal."
  "I thought you told me you were a widow," the salesman replied. "I am, but when there was a decision to be made, my husband and I always made it together. I went into the bedroom and talked with him in Heaven and he said it wasn't for me. The salesman nodded, had a mournful look on his face then got up and said, "Excuse me," then *HE* went into the bedroom, stayed five minutes and returned. "I talked with your husband too. He said you didn't understand the

financing and that you should take the deal!"

Don't think that a car salesman won't do likewise. I've had salesman kneel and pray aloud with a customer promising the lowest price in the United States. He offered the customer $500 cash if they could get a better deal. The salesman was willing to put that in writing. With a statement as convincing as that, the customer bought.

When I questioned the salesman he said he had it covered. If the person wanted to match the deal or beat it, they'd have to buy *two* cars; the deal he would give them and another deal. Nobody would buy two cars to win a $500 bet.

When salesmen hear, "As little as possible." (Some customers say that and smile as if it were an original saying.)

I trained my salespeople to choose an obviously high price like, "Oh, you want to spend around $600 a month?" "Oh no!" they reply, "I was thinking maybe $350." Now the salesman has something to work with.

From experience, when a person demands a very low price, a salesman would first determine if that person *really* wanted that car. Then, turn the question around. "Do you mean that if I offered to sell you this car for $10,000 you'd buy it right now?" Both of us knew it couldn't possibly be bought for that amount.

The customer would greedily say, "Yes." Then the salesman would say, "Let me go check with the manager. Write me a check for the down payment." The salesman would then accept the check. No matter how ridiculous the price was, he would present the deal to the manager, who check the profit margin and keep the check. The manager would ignore the customers figure, start at list price and convert it to a payment. The manager would then write, "OK DEAL at so much a month..." which of course, is substantially higher than $10,000.

The salesman returns to the customer with"the manager's pencil." (What the manager wrote back to the customer.) When the customer sees this, if the monthly payment is what they can afford, they are on the way to owning a new car. The price of the car, now, is unimportant. Once a salesman gets that customer to write a check, he's made a "mental decision" to purchase. He's in a car-buying mode. If the customer balks at the final tally, even with the affordable monthly payment, they just go back and forth until a mutual agreement is made.

On a trade-in, here's how it goes. First, you know I don't recommend you trade in your present car on a new one. Sell it outright. Because of the rebates and cash allowances, the dealer can "mask" the trade in price which is *always* substantially less. That's why new dealerships have used car departments. Remember, their sworn duty is to buy (or trade) for substantially less than the vehicle is worth and then sell for substantially more!

But, for whatever reason you want to trade, this is the way it works. The salesman will take you to the used car manager. The manager will walk around your car with you, subtlely pointing out minor and major defects. The best way to devaluate the vehicle in a customers mind is when they see a dent, to reach down, touch, and go, "Hmmm!" With enough "hmmm's," the customer will begin to think—and sweat!

Then the manager gets in the vehicle, starts it up and with

the customer outside the vehicle, puts one foot on the gas and one on the brake, gives it a little gas, drops it in reverse and you'll hear a loud clunk. You hear this even on new cars if it's done right. And the used car manager *knows* how to do this.

With the door open, he lets the customer hear another "hmmmm." By now, the customer is near quiet panic and is substantially convinced his vehicle has major problems. Then the used car manager gets in to drive the car either around the block where he stops in the parts department to get a cup of coffee, while the customer waits, fidgeting and thinking how little his car is worth.

The used car manager drives back with the new car manager who has a pad and pencil in his hand. About this time, the salesman whom you made the initial contact with, drives up in your new car. They all get out at the same time and sort of surround you. The new car manager shows you his appraisal pad with that big ACV $2000 marked with that crayon. You begin to really sweat. Then, the new car manager raises his hand, adds the (normal) factory rebate, throws in that $500 "cushion", shows you that your trade-in vehicle is now worth $3,500. You rush to sign the agreement faster than you ever realized you could move.

Sweet selling, huh? You have just been *had* yet you are thrilled about it.

If your car is worth between $10,000-$12,000, they grab a figure out of thin air, maybe $7,500. Regardless of the actual worth of your trade-in vehicle. This is done every day in the car business—successfully.

Again, a trade-in is best sold before the customer goes to the dealership.

Let's suppose you have a $5,000 figure in your mind and the salesman breaks out that N.A.D.A. guide and goes down the list you with you and, sure enough, your car is still worth $5,000.

Then he goes to Roman Numeral III, which is the high-mileage deduction in the front of this official book. You'll gasp when you see that your car, which you value at $5,000 now has to *subtract* for this high mileage and it brings you down to what? You guessed it, **ACV $2,000!**

That high-mileage is brutal as well as accurate. Now, when they add the factory rebate and that added $500, you begin to salivate like Pavlov's dog, you're so pleased.

If you do complain even after you've seen the actual worth of your car, they have more answers for you. "You can try selling through the newspapers," they'll say. "Of course, we don't know if this car will be here when you come back because they're selling fast." They always sell fast regardless if they have a hundred just like it that have been on their reserve lot for months. They *said* it was the only one they had.

Before you think about the newspaper ad again, if you're a man, they might have held back that $500 and just offered you $,3000 (ACV $2,000 and Factory Rebate of $1,000) and then throw in that $500 they planned to throw in anyway had you hesitated. Remember, their job is to buy for as little as . . . well you already know that.

If you're a woman and mention putting an ad in the newspaper, you will hear a series of stories about what happens to many people when they "advertise to the world" that they are selling their car. A call and a few seemingly innocent questions can determine when you aren't home for a possible robbery. "You can't trust anybody nowadays." Hey! Scare tactics work!

"What happens far too often," is one of the three men standing over you will say is, "You put an ad in the paper, you get a call from someone inquiring about your car, you invite them to your home (that you know is safe). One car drives up with a single person in it while you have your husband, boyfriend or father there as extra protection. While you and your 'protection' are with the potential buyer, a second car drives up with 4 thugs in it and you are then robbed, burglarized, molested or maybe killed. It happens every day."

The other two salesmen are looking down at the ground and shaking their heads on cue. Then, one of the three will have a bright idea. "Maybe we can throw in another $500 on a used car allowance?" This brings that ACV of $2,000 up to $3,500. Nine out of ten people go for this!

"Or," they'll tell you, "You can sell it in the newspaper but our experience has been that when people do this, their telephone rings all the time. You might only have to show the vehicle to a dozen or more people." As they all smile on cue.

"You might have to take off work, miss a few evenings out, and invariably hear, 'What's the least you'll take for it?' or 'Is this your best price?' Drudgery is what I call it," the person talking says while the other two bow their heads and shake them. They are as practiced as a Las Vegas chorus line. It's their job, don't fault them for it.

They have a ton of frightening stories they will share with you to get you to trade. They'll tell you about the problems you might have with the title transfer at the bank, the taxes the person will squeal over when they have to pay them, the fact that the car might break in a day or a week or a month and the buyer calls back to see what you plan to do about it, or threatens to sue.

Many dealers play a game with you. One big dealership that I knew of had an absolutely horrible looking vehicle on their back lot that should have been used as an artificial reef where they would take customers who wanted the "best deal they could make." It was used as a joke to help "break the ice" between customer and salesperson.

Another customer who read my book said they went to three dealerships and got the lowest price from a salesperson they liked. Then they walked. She returned two days later with her husband who wanted them to knock an additional $500 off the price.

Of course, this *nice* salesman who had turned you over (TO'ed) to his manager, who is much more experienced in this negotiating business, gave you a price. When your nice salesman returned, regardless of how highly outrageous the price might have been, are taught to say "Whew! You really got a good deal. I've never seen one so low. You must have said the right things." Every salesman is taught to say that. It makes the customer feel that they, without doubt, did get a good deal.

So the lady came back with her husband who wanted an additional $500 off and the sales manager wouldn't budge. They walked. When they were getting into their car, the nice salesperson bolted out of the door and yelled, "Wait! I can't believe it but you've got the deal!"

That, is smart bargaining! The dealership still made

money but you got the best deal possible. If you are willing to walk and they let you, perhaps the deal was not at all good for the dealership. Then, you go to yet another dealership. This time you have had at least one practice which doubles your chances of not getting taken unfair advantage of.

One of the dealerships, trust me, will not let you walk. If that extra $500 savings is important to you, go for it. Remember, we're talking about money and $500 will buy a nice weekend vacation for you or that first set of tires that need to be replaced.

Options. Of course, they will option you to death. You saw that 25,000 car after they took the options. And the fact is, I didn't really start. The higher-priced cars come with standard things like automatic trans, power steering, AC, nice radio and tape player, maybe a CD, dual air bags, expensive wheel covers, power steering, power brakes, seats, windows, trunk lock. The auto dealers have found a way of eliminating a salesman failing to sell you these options and put them on anyway and, of course, charge you for them. But, as you know, there are many, many, MANY options that aren't on many, many, MANY cars and if you listen to the salesperson, you'll buy them all.

I have a friend who is really tight with the buck. He looked in the newspaper at a dealership ad for a new bottom-of-the line Toyota pick up advertised for $5,842. He checked in Consumer Guide, another way to get factory invoice price, and decided that he wanted that truck.

He walked into the dealership, was greeted by a salesperson and pointed to the ad. Do you still have one of those, any color will do? The salesman said they did and my friend, Eddie, said he wanted it.

Then came the options. "Uh, Sir," the salesman said, "It doesn't have a radio. But I can put one in for you, with tape deck and our best speakers for . . . "

"No radio," Eddie said, "I'll hum."

The salesman smiled.

"We have an extended warranty and I can get that for you for. . . " Eddie raised his hand, motioning the salesman to halt. "It has a 3-year 36,000 mile warranty, I will just drive if for three years and sell it, and I won't drive over 10,000 miles per year. I don't need it."

The salesman continued, "There is this rust proofing that I can offer you for. . . " Eddie held up his hand again. "Do you mean that this truck will rust? Isn't that covered in the 3-year 36,000 mile thing?"

"Well, yes it is. But to be extra sure. . ."

"I'm sure I don't want it." Eddie cut in.

"Uh, Sir, the truck we listed doesn't have any side mirrors and those are only . . ."

Up went the hand again. "It has a rear view mirror, doesn't it?"

"Yes."

"Then that's all I'll need. If I have to see better I'll turn around or lean over."

"Sir, the clock is not standard in this model. For $175 . . ."

Up went the hand again. "I'll tape a Timex on the dashboard."

By this time the salesman was convinced that he was not going to get a cent out of Eddie. He decided he'd stick it to him on the financing and the credit life. But, of course, that didn't happen. Eddie had a cashiers check in his hand already made out to the dealership for $5,842. And do you know what? He drove out in the truck. Oh, he had to write a check for taxes, title and license, but he was a salesman's nightmare!

Every once in a while, he drives by the dealership, honks his horn and waves to the salesman and the sales manager. They smile, shake their heads, laugh and wave back. They respected Eddie and they liked him.

There was another time when a guy came in while I was working in the finance office. I loaded him up with credit life, accident & health, extended service policy, etc. This guy came in thinking $250 or $300 a month.

I would always hit them with a real high payment to begin with. It would blow their mind and I could sign them up for $350 or $400 per month with ease.

This guy came in to sign up and get a new pickup truck. When I told him his payments would be $848 per month. His eyes got about as big as saucers, he rocked back in his chair and almost fell over. After reeling around, he looked at the contract, grabbed my pen and as he signed the papers he said, "Well, I'll try them for a little while."

I felt so sorry for him, I let him off the hook.

THE SALES PROCESS

A salesperson generally has 10 steps to follow to get you to buy a vehicle:

✓Approach—Meet and greet the prospect promptly and in a friendly manner.

✓Find Common Grounds—Get to know the prospect.

✓Qualify—Determine how much money the prospect has to spend, right now!

✓Land on a Specific Vehicle In Stock—A vehicle that meets the prospect's needs, wants and price range.

✓Present That Vehicle—Give the prospect a bumper-to-bumper presentation—Explain all of the features and benefits to the prospect.

✓Demonstrate That Vehicle—Get the prospect to drive the vehicle.

✓Re-evaluate—Overcome all objections— Ask the prospect, "If the price is right, will you buy today?", "Why not?" Examine the trade-in.

✓Write the Deal—Assume the purchase—Start at full list price—Manufacturer's suggested retail price—Appraise trade-in—Start at actual cash value or less.

✓Close the Deal—Negotiate to a price, payment or difference that the prospect will buy now, no matter how ridiculous. Ask for the down payment or cash.

✓ Turn Over To Management—At any point during the sale that the prospect believably indicates that a sale cannot be completed today, get a manager involved.

By the time most people go through this process with a true professional, they will drive off in a new vehicle that they paid top dollar for. Having knowledge of the dealer's game-plan allows you to take advantage of the opportunity to get a better deal.

No matter how you go about buying a new car, you will have to deal with a salesperson somewhere along the way. I say, listen to what they say and let them do their job. Use their expertise to find out about the car you are interested in purchasing. When it's time to really get "down to brass tacks" you, now, have the hammer!

Most people only let themselves walk around the lot, looking at the *outside* of the cars, through the window at the interior, get scared at the sticker price, ask for a brochure and go home with that molested feeling. But you, now (or when you finish this book) know that you don't have to do anything that you don't want to. Accept the friendly service and take the vehicle on a test drive.

Ask about manufacturer's incentive options, ask for a brochure, state that you aren't ready to buy now as you haven't investigated other brands yet. Take notes. Ask for the salesperson's card. If he (she) did a good job and you decide on that model, be sure to ask for that salesperson, if you return to that dealership.

Don't be concerned with your ability to get the best deal elsewhere. I'll teach you to get the best deal here! Your principal considerations at this point are, selecting the right vehicle, selecting the right dealership for later service convenience and/or reputation, and exploring your options.

You know your needs in a vehicle as far as size, type, number of doors, carrying capacity, image, fuel economy, etc. You should list them. Of course, if your family is going to share this vehicle, get their input. Now, write down everything you and your family want:

NEW CAR SPECS

Size	Type
# of Doors	Fuel Economy
Capacity	Image
Transmission	Power

Required Options :

_____
_____
_____

Desired Options:

_____
_____
_____
_____

Make it a point to look at all manufacturer's vehicles with dealers in your area. You might find vehicles, you haven't considered, may meet your criteria. If you are concerned with buying American, the country of origin and percentage of parts produced in the United States are now posted on all vehicles. You might be surprised at how many with Japanese names are produced in America and at how many

American names are produced overseas. With assembly lines operated by robotics, you will find quality and consistency fairly equal across the board. Of course engineering and class are still distinguishable.

By all means, accept the presentations and demonstrations from the salespeople. They are trained to know these vehicles well. You'll gain valuable information about the vehicles you look at, and learn about things that can't be found in brochures or publications.

If you find that you don't like a particular salesperson for any reason(s), don't judge the dealership by that individual. Feel free to ask for a different person to help you. I once had a lady customer tell me that she didn't think that we could get along, and nicely asked if I would get her another salesperson. Amazingly enough, I wasn't enjoying her company either.

I knew a salesman that reminded me of her and introduced them. She bought from him. To my surprise, when we met again a couple of months later in the service department, she referred a customer to me. I don't exactly know where the "car salesman" got such a bad reputation. They are as diverse in personality as any group I've experienced. Partake of their services, they're one of the few things that are still free . . . until you buy.

ADVERTISING

Take it as fact—all advertising does is get you to come to the dealership. I mentioned earlier that every dealer, whether he buys 20 cars or 2,000, gets the exact same price! I also recall telling you somewhere near the front of the book, that if you have a dealership next to the manufacturing plant and another dealer has his on the farthest end of Key West, the cost of that vehicle to each dealer is the same.

It is not uncommon for a dealer to have one and only one vehicle that they advertise for a certain price in the news-paper. This way they can avoid problems with the Sate Motor Vehicle Commission or the Better Business Bureau or any Consumer Fraud agency that seem to pop up here and there, usually championed by a local, ambitious television newsman trying to climb the ladder to anchor.

Some states let you get away with this. In Texas, for example, the rules for auto advertising are extremely explicit and sternly enforced. If you only have one vehicle on sale, you have to specify that you have, in fact, only one vehicle at that price.

I see ads daily in the newspaper and over television and hear them over the radio about a gigantic end-of-the-month sale or inventory sale, or going out-of-business sale or fire sale or any cutesy name the dealer's PR Department can dream up and all of the sales are . . . bull puckey!

One dealer I knew of, had almost all inventory severely damaged after a monstrous hail storm. After the insurance company settled with him, they ran a Dimpled Darling Sale. People came out in droves to buy these slightly dented vehicles. So many people came out for this *deal*, that many of the vehicles were purchased for a higher price than they sold for before the storm! The dealer dented most of his newly arriving inventory with a hammer to keep the influx coming.

Another dealer says he apologizes to his competition for selling cars so cheap, but he loves people and wants to make everybody a great deal. This is B.S. too.

Most of the deals you'll see advertised in the newspaper are the most stripped down vehicles of that particular car line that the dealership can order. Some offer cars without air conditioning. Some have manual transmissions. "Leader cars" are advertised to beat the competition. Dealers really don't want to sell this car. It's the "main attraction" as well as the old "bait and switch" routine. You probably wouldn't want it either because the most common color of leader cars is "Exorcist Pea Soup Green." They get you there at one price, then go to work on you for another price on a different car.

The best thing to do is to ignore those stories and ploys that the sales people try on you. All you want to accomplish is select the vehicle that you want. Just ask them to show you the cars.

Of course, if the vehicle you want is a 1999 Testosterone with a 983 HP V-42 with a semi-automatic 15-speed tyranny, you won't find many competitive makes. With over 58 different name plates to choose from, and each has a minimum of 5 different models, each model has say . . . 3 option groups, and 6 additional options, not to mention the 10 choices of color, that would give you over 52,200 vehicles to look at and you would still have to choose an engine and transmission on each. It could get pretty overwhelming.

Narrow your choices down to your favorite few. That's why some of the best advice I can offer is to rent one for a few days or a full week to make certain you're going to be happy with your choice.

One customer, in order to try to decide which truck to buy, would sit in the service department's customer lounge and talk to disgruntled new vehicle owners at different dealerships. He would tell me some of their stories from time to time. It took him almost three years to build up the courage to buy anything. His old truck finally "laid down" on him and he had no choice.

I suppose you could get too analytical when selecting a vehicle. It's a big decision. It's probably as difficult to make a good one as it is to make a bad one. Most all new vehicles are good. It all boils down to, "It's an emotional thing!"

Take your time. It's a big investment and you don't want to be stuck with 5 years to pay for something you're not absolutely happy with. Check out as many vehicles as you like or, if you have your mind made up which model you want, it is time to prepare for getting the best price.

Step 5

THE BEST PRICE

It is often said in the car business that, if you like the car you bought, and you can afford the payments, you got the best deal. That probably applies to the masses that paid more than they should have for their new car. So, what *is* a good deal? It depends on the perspective of the individual involved.

From a dealer's point of view, it's a profitable deal. Some profit margins are more than others. The average gross profit on a typical new car deal is close to $3,000 including finance reserves. Only you and the dealer can determine the profit margin of the deal you get. They like the deal to cost you more and you, like it to cost you less. Now we're getting down to the fun part.

The term Dealer's Cost is ambiguous at best. Many people mistakenly believe that the dealer makes several thousand dollars on each deal. Sometimes they do. More often, they don't. Factory Invoice is what the manufacturer charges the Dealer's Wholesale Floor Plan Account for the vehicle upon delivery to the dealer. The dealer then accrues daily interest on that floor plan amount. The actual cost of a vehicle increases every day the vehicle remains unsold.

The dealership's operating expenses, often quite substantial, are not figured into the costing of the vehicle by the sales department personnel. The operating expense for the dealership is taken from the gross of all the departments combined; service, body shop, parts, new and used vehicle sales, and finance and insurance.

Most manufacturers refund the dealer, on average, 3% of the Manufacturer's Suggested Retail Price quarterly for each vehicle sold. There are also other additional dealer incentives that apply to slower-moving vehicles. Perhaps you're familiar with the frequently announced consumer rebates and rate incentives from the manufacturers. Therefore, the actual cost the dealer pays for a vehicle is not easily determined; other factors apply, such as, supply and demand and just "Good 'ole American Capitalism".

It is difficult for us to dictate what a dealer will accept as a minimal profit since we cannot accurately determine what that cost is to that dealer. We can't even make an educated guess on what a dealer will accept as a profit on an automobile because far too many outside factors apply, such as a dealers overhead and expenses, competition, and economic climate.

I mentioned earlier that all dealers pay the same amount for their vehicles regardless of the size of their dealership, the amount of cars they buy, or their location in reference to the factory from which their vehicles are delivered. The

MSRP and Factory Invoice is the same for all identically equipped vehicles anywhere in the country (New York has unique warranty compliance laws that increase their cost a bit).

The Factory Invoice is a commonly accepted point of reference in all wholesale transactions of new vehicles. Dealers buying vehicles from other dealers almost always pay Factory Invoice to each other. Generally, this is the reference point accepted as *cost* for a vehicle. It is not, however, the actual cost to the dealer.

It is not uncommon for a dealer to disclose the Factory Invoice to a prospect intent on buying a vehicle. As a rule the copies are accurate and can be accepted as authentic. If you are not the trusting type, you can do your own research and calculate the amount yourself.

SOURCES: NEW VEHICLE PRICING INFO

You can accurately obtain the Factory Invoice Price from several sources as long as these sources are current. I suggest you check with your local bookstore for **Consumer Reports**. They publish a guide that is fairly detailed for most vehicles and also give you other information, such as their opinion as to the quality and durability of many cars.

A second book to look in is **Edmund's New Car Prices.** Edmund's publishes a series of books and you can find the one that relates to the vehicle you are interested in buying. A similar book is one put out by **Pace Publications**. They also publish a series of books, Again, look into the one that tells about your particular vehicle.

FACTORY INVOICE WORKSHEET

MSRP   Factory Inv.

Year _____ Make _____
Model _____ Style _____
Engine . . . .
Transmission . . . .
Base Price . . . .
Preferred Equipment Group # . . . .
Name of Package _____

Options Included in Package:

Package Additional Discount _____ minus . . . .

+ Options:

+ Transportation Charge

= Total Price of Vehicle:

Be advised that your ability to get an exact calculation is sometimes difficult, due to frequent manufacturer's price increases. Often the sources at your disposal may be somewhat outdated. Check for the most recent updates. There are several publications that are on the market in both book form and software for PC's. A trip to your local library or book store will probably get you just what you need.

If you have access to a credit union, most have methods for Factory Invoice calculations. Some banks can also be helpful. If your dealer is adamant that your calculation is incorrect, be sure that you have added the transportation charge. A common mistake many people make is failure to add this charge. The transportation charge is disclosed on the window sticker and must be added to the price of the Factory Invoice.

Be careful with discount packages. If you don't read your guide book (Edmund's, Pace, Consumer Reports) correctly, you could accidentally charge yourself for free options and end up with a Factory Invoice that might be quite high. Give yourself a margin for error, maybe a couple of hundred dollars. If the dealer's Factory Invoice copy is close, accept it. It is probably correct.

> *Armed with a Factory Invoice you should be able to obtain your vehicle within a few hundred dollars of Factory Invoice.*

One rule-of-thumb that might prove helpful, especially when trying to find a vehicle that fits in your price range, is Factory Invoice will often be between 85% and 90% of the MSRP or "Window Sticker": Use the 85% figure. There are many cases where this is not exactly true, since Factory Invoice is occasionally more than this, especially on the lower-priced models, maybe 5% more. On top-of-the-line cars, Factory Invoice could be less, probably 5% less.

When negotiating with your dealer, keep in mind that current market conditions affect the pricing of your new car/truck/van. Also know that your salesperson will probably earn around 25% of the amount over Factory Invoice that you pay.

If for some reason you can't negotiate a sales price that you think is fair, or if you are meek and don't have the stomach for negotiating, call the "Fleet Manager" at the dealership. Don't tell him that you've been there, just describe the car you want and ask him if he would sell it for your figure. He will either agree to sell it or tell you that he can't. More than likely, he'll quote you a good low price in keeping with market conditions.

FACTORY ORDER

If you prefer to *factory-order* the exact vehicle you want, the Fleet Manager is probably the only person you should deal with. I've seen many people in fits of rage, having to wait as long as six weeks after ordering a vehicle from an inexperienced salesperson, only to find out that the vehicle was either improperly ordered, or was not available with the options they requested.

It is not at all uncommon for a dealer to "Locate" the exact vehicle you want. Keep in mind that a purchase from another dealer involves increased cost, because part of the money the dealership earns (3% of the Manufacturer's Suggested Retail Price paid to the dealer who ordered the car from the manufacturer)goes to the dealer that supplies the car. Your dealership can get the exact car you want from another dealer, somewhere, at Factory Invoice, but the dealer who sold the car (to the other dealer) gets the 3%.There might also be a time and transportation charge.

One time I went from Texas to Oklahoma to get the car a customer demanded. He paid extra. He paid cost of time and transportation and 3% more than what he would have had he chosen a car from my lot. Finding the exact car on the lot at the price you want to pay has it's rewards. The question is now, *how do you pay for it?*

Step 6

FINANCING

Very few people have the means to pay cash for a new vehicle. Even if they do, at today's interest rates, they may be able to find investments that would yield more benefits than the interest they would pay. Most people finance their purchase. Being knowledgeable about financing will help you save even more money.

Financing a vehicle can be complex. There are many more options today than in recent years. Extended terms up to 72 months are now common on higher-priced vehicles. Attractive leasing options are available. Balloon payment contracts offer alternatives to leasing that are worthy of consideration. There are *First Time Buyers Plans, College Graduate Plans, Special Finance Plans,* and I'm sure, more to come.

Normal financing for the "credit worthy" is the simplest to negotiate. You can easily shop rate at your bank, credit union and your dealership. Most dealerships have many lending sources available. The now common, "Simple Interest Contracts" allow for a faster reduction of principle than the old manner of calculation.

Try negotiating the rate with your dealer. They can usually be competitive and often get you a lower rate than you can get elsewhere. You might find it advantageous financing through the dealership to reserve your credit line at your credit union or bank for emergencies. A national credit rating with a manufacturer's lending institution is an extremely valuable asset when applying for other loans.

Interest rates are usually graded by a computer that judges three criteria; (1) Ability, (2) Stability, and (3) Willingness. Each of these qualifications are assessed and graded to calculate a probability of payment, called a Risk Score, which determines your categorization into a Tier system. These Tiers are usually set in classifications with the letters A, B, C, and D. Anything less than "D" results in a denial of extension of credit. The interest rate that you will be able to obtain improves as you elevate your score toward the "A".

A Credit Application or Customer Statement is the key to getting a good score. As you may recall, I stated that you are graded by a computer. The information requested on the application counts as points. I'm sure you've heard the old adage, "Garbage in—garbage out". This is unfortunately true in this case.

Neatness of the information on the application is almost as important as the completeness of it. The application is typically faxed to the lending institution where an input clerk, who usually has a large stack of applications to handle, types all the information on the application into a computer.

> *Helpful Hint: Use black ink. Blue ink does not fax well. Good information may not transmit legibly.*

If the information is not legible, the clerk simply leaves it blank. No information input, no score tabulated for that information. Minor details such as missing area codes or zip codes are enough to downgrade an offering from "A" to "B". This could cost you a few hundred dollars over a 60-month contract. Be neat and write or print legibly!

One area of heavy emphasis in scoring an application is references. All lending institutions ask for the names, (complete) addresses, and telephone numbers of a few relatives and friends. They use this information to help locate you if you become delinquent in your payments and/or move. If you leave the state, you realize, you are still obligated to pay your car loan. Lack of this information makes it more difficult to collect and therefore an increased rate is called for to offset the expense. Thorough, complete, legible information can save you another few hundred dollars.

ABILITY

Let's examine the three criteria for grading. First, "Ability" is a measure of how you plan to pay your new payment. We have discussed your Gross Monthly Income. Here, you establish a *Debt-to-Income-Ratio*. You have to earn enough money to afford your payment. You can enhance your Ability score also, by offering a larger down payment. Cash down payment, as opposed to Trade-In Allowance indicates to the computer that you can save money. This shows additional Ability to pay.

Your spouse's income is often necessary to reduce your debt-to-income ratio. The lending institution's computer automatically pulls at least one of your credit bureau reports to further define your open credit balances and payment obligations.

Be sure to advise the financial analyst that you have sold and paid off your trade-in vehicle since your credit bureau file may not have had time to indicate that fact. Additional income, if you have any, is an asset if you can prove it. One area often overlooked is monthly rent for those with roommates. You should list only the part of the rent that you are responsible for.

If both you and your spouse are on the application, don't list the mortgage payment under both applicants, put it on the principle buyer and write under the co-buyer, "Lives with spouse". Otherwise, the computer might misjudge your debt-to-income and again, cost you hundreds of dollars in non-tax deductible interest.

STABILITY

"Stability" is graded by your length of time in both your residence and employment. Little attention is paid to previous residence and employment by most lenders. The computer scores *zero* for sparse or incomplete information. Long-time current residence and long-time previous residence is a fine indicator for probability of payment. A short-term current residence does not disqualify you, but combine it with a long-term *previous* residence to markedly improve your stability score.

Truthfulness is also important in this area. Your residence

history is on your credit bureau report. You might examine your report to see if all previous residences are listed. Your employment history is as important as residence history, although it is not as often updated in your credit bureau file. Too, remember to be complete with area codes, telephone numbers, street addresses, city, state and zip codes.

For those of you who consider yourself self-employed, take note that lenders often consider an application with "Self-Employed" listed as employment, makes the offering a Commercial Account. Many lenders aren't interested in these accounts. They frequently limit the term of these contracts to 24 or 36 months.

What I'd prefer you do, is list the name of your company as your employer, list your occupation as "Owner" or "President" and then put down your name as your supervisor. There are three different spaces on this application and remember, the *computer* may score your information better and get longer term financing, especially on your personal vehicle.

WILLINGNESS

"Willingness" is a misnomer. It is a measure of how you have paid your bills in the past. This information is almost exclusively obtained from your credit bureau report. They report how many times you have been 30, 60, or 90 days late making payments. The more *on time* your payments are, the better your report is perceived. If you are currently past due on one or several loans, you can almost be assured of a denial. If you have had difficulties in the past and have been current for a year or two, your chances are real good that you may be forgiven. You may not grade "A" then again, you may.

Lenders are more lenient than ever before in recorded history; especially manufacturer's lending institutions who lend money on their own make vehicles.

Another way to improve willingness with a lender is by making a larger cash down payment. With more cash down, you demonstrate two very important factors to a lender. One, is that they would rather loan less on the vehicle than it's value. In the event of a repossession, their losses will be either eliminated or greatly lessened.

The second, is that by having a larger investment in the vehicle, you are less likely to just *walk away* from it in the event it has serious mechanical problems or you opt to put your car payment on a new boat. Without the car, there is no way to trailer the boat so, you need that car.

If your credit is questionable, I advise you to examine your credit report at your local credit bureau. It might save you more than the couple of dollars it will cost to get a copy of your report. Should the report not be to your liking and you feel they have incorrect information, you can demand that this information be removed. The burden of proof is on the reporting agency.

What this means is, let's suppose you took an extended vacation and you were late on a payment to Sears and they reported it to the credit bureau. First, I'd call the credit manager at Sears, explain why you were late, show them that you've been a loyal customer for 12 years, tell them you plan on buying a new car, and show them your credit report, assuming of course, you don't have a dozen black marks on it. If so, forget it and know that you'll have to put down a *substantial down payment* to get any loan. Chances are high that they will call the credit bureau and have it removed.

Some department stores and credit card companies have computers that *automatically* report even mildly delinquent accounts to the credit bureau, but the credit manager can have them removed. If the credit manager is a "snit" and refuses or says he can't do this, then go to the credit bureau.

One word of caution: A *letter or comment* that you write to the Credit Bureau is usually posted on your file and every potential lender sees it. Avoid posting a comment. A credit history will eventually be deleted but the comment stays!

It is important that any negative information be removed because it could hamper your chances of getting financing and if not, you'll certainly have to pay more interest and more of a down payment.

If you find incorrect information, ask the bureau to contact the reporting agency and have it corrected. It is not uncommon to find your file mixed up with someone with the same name, if your name is Johnson, Jackson, Smith, Jones, etc. The credit bureau information is much more accurate than in the past, but mistakes are still made.

If you have never financed a vehicle before, you can still obtain financing. Many manufacturers now have special programs for first-time buyers. They will be more apt to lend on one of what they call "entry-level" vehicles. (Ford Escort, Chevy Cavalier, Honda Civic); cars that are, for the most part, the least expensive, and fuel efficient to maintain their C.A.F.E. (Corporate Average Fuel Economy) rating for the Government (EPA).

First time buyers, don't set your standards too high, because you haven't proven that you are a good credit risk and conversely, neither have you proven that you are a bad credit risk.

Also, first time buyers, expect to have some equity in your new vehicle. In other words, you might have to put down a larger down payment until such time as you prove that you are, in fact, not a credit risk. Most lenders will not accept any derogatory credit on a young buyer.

Lenders do, however, love first time buyers who are college graduates working in their field. Often they will offer special low interest rates and rebates. Be sure to inquire about their college grad plan to see if you qualify.

Perhaps the easiest way to get a car if you are a first time buyer is with a *co-signer*. It usually is limited to a parent. The lending institutions have better luck getting a parent to pay, in the event of default by a son or daughter.

I have included below, a worksheet to help you gather the information that you'll need to properly complete a good credit application. Fill this out and take it with you for reference.

CREDIT APPLICATION INFORMATION

Name as it appears on your driver's license:

Residence Telephone Number (Area Code):

Social Security #

Current Street Address: (Street, City, State, Zip)

_____

_____

Previous Street Address: (Street, City, State, Zip)

_____

_____

Previous Street Address: (Street, City, State, Zip)

_____

_____

_____
Current Employer's Company Name

_____
Street, City, State, Zip

_____
Your Supervisor's Name/ Telephone Number (Area Code)

_____
Previous Employer's Company Name

_____
Street, City, State, Zip

_____
Your Ex-Supervisor's Name/Telephone Number (Area Code)

_____
Previous Employer's Company Name

_____
Street, City, State, Zip

_____
Your Ex-Supervisor's Name/Telephone Number (Area Code)

Your Bank or Credit Union Name _____
Checking Account # _____ Savings Account # _____
Telephone Number (Area Code) _____

_____
Name of Your Closest Relative (not living with you)
_____
Address (Street, City, State, Zip)
_____
Telephone Number (Area Code)

_____
Name of Another Relative (not living with you)
_____
Address (Street, City, State, Zip)
_____
Telephone Number (Area Code)

_____
Name of Another Relative (not living with you)
_____
Address (Street, City, State, Zip)
_____
Telephone Number (Area Code)

_____
Name of A Personal Friend (not living with you)
_____
Address (Street, City, State, Zip)
_____
Telephone Number (Area Code)

Name of A Personal Friend (not living with you)

Address (Street, City, State, Zip)

Telephone Number (Area Code)

Name of A Personal Friend (not living with you)

Address (Street, City, State, Zip)

Telephone Number (Area Code)

Last Vehicle Financed by

Address (Street, City, State, Zip)

Telephone Number (Area Code)

Account Number   Date Paid   # and Amount of Payments

Previous Vehicle Financed by

Address (Street, City, State, Zip)

Telephone Number (Area Code)

Account Number   Date Paid   # and Amount of Payments

Insurance Company

Name of Your Insurance Agent

Address (Street, City, State, Zip)

Telephone Number (Area Code)

Policy Number   Effective Date   Expires

With this information, you can accurately complete a customer statement at the dealership, your bank, or credit union. It is also a good idea to take along copies of your driver's license, social security card, auto insurance policy and your paycheck stubs or other proof of income. It will shorten the amount of time it takes to get an answer, thus insuring your qualification for the lowest possible interest rate.

Another word of caution: Do not apply for a loan everywhere you go, and do not sign anything allowing someone to pull your credit bureau report until you are ready to purchase your new vehicle. Inquiries on your credit bureau are registered each time you allow someone to pull a report. Some lenders may misjudge your intentions with a lot of inquiries. I've seen them turn down a perfectly good individual due to numerous inquiries. Their logic is that, you could be buying a vehicle at each place you go. They have, on several occasions, unknowingly financed fleets of vehicles on an individual's credit rating, who was trying to open a new company (bad risk).

To this point we have discussed general conventional financing. What about . . .

ALTERNATIVE FINANCING

If you can't qualify for a conventional loan, you can probably still get financed for a vehicle. Maybe not a new one, maybe so. I'm sure, by now, you have seen the "Good Credit—Bad Credit—No Credit" advertisements. Essentially, they are lenders that will take a risk at the highest legal interest rate. They require a bit more documentation, but if you are at the "Wheels are Better than Heels" point of need, what choice do you have?

Using one of these options, you can begin to re-establish your credit with one of these lenders. As a rule, those "Buy Here—Pay Here" lots do not report your payment history to any credit bureau. Their intention is to keep you as a captive customer - forever! There are now many banks that offer "Second Chance" type financing through auto dealers. Many charge fees, paid by the dealer, to finance a vehicle for you.

If you have a bad credit history, be prepared to have a good-sized down payment and, chances are, the price of the vehicle is non-negotiable! You are now *paying* for your mistakes or misdeeds! If (when) you do get this alternative financing even at a higher percentage rate, you then are able to re-establish your credit at the credit bureau.

Again, either by bad luck or bad money handling, you put yourself in this position. So, don't fault the lender or the dealership. They have rules. On the bright side, if you have made a mistake, you won't be faulted for it for the rest of your life.

If you are in this higher risk group, prepare yourself by having copies of your telephone bills (in your name). "No Phone—No Loan" is usually the rule. They often require a letter of residence from your landlord, and a letter of explanation of your past credit problems.

You might also make a list of five relatives and five friends as listed on the previous pages. They usually want a minimum of five years residence history and five years employment history. With this data, you can most likely get dependable, late-model transportation, if not new. Check them out if your situation applies. You might be very pleasantly surprised. Don't give up!

For the more credit worthy there are the *Smart Buy, Gold Key Plus, Customer Option Plan, Leadership Purchase Plan,* and too many others to name. All are similar in concept and merit consideration. Basically they are finance agreements with *Guaranteed Residual Balloon Notes*. Nobody has really come up with an across-the-board accepted name for these contracts.

An example of a "Balloon Note" is: If you are trying to buy a car for, $20,000 and you want low monthly payments for, two years because you are a young businessman and chances are that, within two years, you'll be making much more money, they might finance only $10,000 of that $20,000 for you to pay on a monthly basis and at the end of the two years, your "balloon note" of $10,000 is due. If, at the end of two years, you still don't have the money, you can again get financing on the $10,000 balance.

Manufacturers like balloon note financing for several reasons. First, it shortens the trading cycle so they can sell more vehicles. A balloon note is an alternative to 7-year financing, which may become a necessity if the cost of vehicles continue to rise as they have in the recent past. Second, they are under the impression that balloon notes will lead to increased customer satisfaction and owner loyalty. You see, if your financing is only for 2 or 3 years, you will turn the car in before it is out of warranty. Third, balloon notes help sell more vehicles because of the lower payments. Many manufacturers are subsidizing rates, enhancing residuals and offering huge rebates on these plans.

With a balloon note, the usual term for a new car loan is 24 or 36 months. At the end of the term you have three choices:

✓You can simply **turn the vehicle in** with preplanned mileage and reasonable wear and tear and/or pay for excessive wear and tear. If it's minor, you might lose only your security deposit. But, if you've wrecked it or the transmission is grinding, you are responsible.

✓You can **refinance** the balance and theoretically maintain essentially the same payment.

✓You can **pay off the balance** in full. You see, your payment has "ballooned".

I recommend exploring these options BEFORE you commit to a 60-month contract.

If you go for one of these plans, check out "Gap" insurance. This guarantees that the lender will be paid in full in the event you total your car or if it is stolen.

LEASING

Leasing began about twenty years ago as a good idea but has not lived up to everyone's expectations. I think the concept was abused by the promotion of leases that ran for 48 months. Four years is a long time to have one car and since so many of these leases were cars driven by traveling salesmen, the cars simply became "old" to them..

Most customers were under the mistaken impression that they could just turn in the vehicle whenever they were ready, and were disappointed to find out that they would have to pay an exorbitant amount just to get out of the lease. It didn't take long for the lease to get a bad reputation. There were no "Guaranteed Residuals." Most of the leases were written as "Open End Leases" where the lessee was responsible for the residual value of the vehicle at lease end.

In other words, a person could lease a car for 48 months, pay a reasonably high lease payment, get a full income tax write-off from it and then when they turned the car back in, find out that they still owed money! Whereas, had they purchased and financed the same car, they may have paid less, had the close to the same tax benefits, and had equity in the car, maybe even owned it outright, at the end of the four years. The leasing companies, in my estimation, were greedy and as it turns out, foolishly greedy.

Leasing today is somewhat different. It's still like renting a vehicle for a fixed period of time. The lease is a calculated method of allowing you to use a vehicle for a term and pay only the depreciation and interest. The value of the vehicle at the end of the lease is based on a percentage of the Manufacturer's Suggested Retail Price of the vehicle. Many manufacturers guarantee this value at the end of the lease.

In most cases a "Closed End Lease" is what is written now. That is, the lessee has no responsibility at lease end except to return the vehicle to the lessor in *normal* (not wrecked or seriously abused) condition and with no more than the specified mileage, determined and agreed upon at the beginning of the lease in the lease contract.

ADVANTAGES OF LEASING

1.   Minimized initial capital outlay: This includes the first month's lease payment and a refundable security deposit which is usually equal to that or, two months in advance.

2.   Lower monthly payments for a shorter term: If you were going to buy a car and finance it for 60 or 72 months, your payments on a 24 or 36 month lease, per month, may be the same or less.

3.   There may be tax advantages for business use: I say "may be" instead of "is" because it depends on how the vehicle is used. It has to be exclusively for business purposes. The government set new rules down in that you cannot buy a snazzy new car, use it to mail a few letters and the rest of the time to impress your relatives and friends and write it off.

4.   There is no asset or liability on a financial statement, it's a monthly expense: If you owned the car, it is an *asset* and all you can write off is the depreciation. A leased vehicle, it is a total business expense and you write off the full amount.

5. You are not committed to the vehicle except for the term of the lease, commonly 24 or 36 months: In other words, if you want a new vehicle at the end of this lease period, you just lease a different one and do not have to hassle with trying to sell or trade in your present vehicle to do so.

6. It doesn't tie up your cash: You will never have your money invested in a vehicle. Your total initial cash outlay is two months rent up front, and you have not used up your credit line. For instance, if you buy a vehicle, and let's say you put 30% down and finance 70%, you should be in a "positive" equity position, that is, you owe less than the value of the vehicle.

Whereas, during the lease period, you are always in a "negative" equity position until the end of the lease at which time you reach "zero" equity. To make it easier to understand, it means that you have your cash in your pocket and not invested in some vehicle.

DISADVANTAGES OF LEASING

1. **Often, your automobile insurance is higher due to additional insureds:** For instance, the lease vehicle is titled in the name of the financing institution. If, for example, you were to crash into a school bus full of children, the owner would face a humongous lawsuit. Thus, the lender requires they be listed on the insurance policy and this costs more. Lenders also require increased liability limits because of the aforementioned example, which you pay for.

2. **There is a charge at lease end for excessive mileage:**

At the beginning of this lease, you sign a contract stating that you will drive a specified number of miles, usually 15,000 miles per year. If, for whatever reason, you drive *over* that amount, you will be charged at a rate of around 15 cents per mile. If you drive *less* than the allotted 15,000 miles, there is *no* credit.

3. The lessor, individual or company that leases you the vehicle, does not have to disclose the capitalized cost of the vehicle or the interest rate charged: What this means is, that when you take out a lease, the lessor does not have to tell you the actual price they are charging you for that vehicle; you know *only* the monthly lease payment. So, they can get more money out of you unless . . . unless you are knowledgeable.

To combat this overcharging, simply find out the selling price of the same vehicle and calculate a payment for 48 months at the going interest rate to purchase. Then, compare this payment with your lease payment for 24 or 36 months. I'd also get the price from a second leasing company and compare the rates. Let me tell you how and why a leasing company can do this.

They can finance up to 115% of the Manufacturer's Suggested Retail Price of the vehicle, tack on a few extra percentage points on the finance charge and add all of that in and charge you, legally, a higher price. Some do it and some do not. With the competition, I doubt if but a few would do this but check anyway if you care, okay?

4.   Be certain to check with the lessor as to any additional property taxes assessed during the lease:

These, you might not become aware of until year end.
Be certain to inquire about these *before* you sign the lease!

5. In the event of a total loss; theft, wrecked, flood or fire, you will owe more than the vehicle is worth: This is where *Gap* insurance comes in handy. It will cost you but it is to protect both you and the lender to cover this difference. Ask about it when you are inquiring about leasing.

With all of these plans to buy or lease a car, which one is best for you? This, of course, depends on your personal situation. For most people who are in a business where leasing is best, I'd recommend you first negotiate the price for a conventional purchase and inquire about a 24 and 36 month *balloon note* based on that price.

After you are given a quote on the balloon note, ask them to prepare a quote on a lease for both 24 and 36 months. Theoretically, the lease *should* be the lowest payment. Just be certain their lease quote includes all taxes in the payments. I, personally, like a 24-month lease. You know exactly what the use of a vehicle will cost on an equal monthly basis, and you will always have late-model, dependable transportation at the lowest cost. There is an old adage that says, "If it appreciates, *BUY IT*! If it depreciates, *LEASE IT*!"

Only you can decide your comfort zone. I have shown you how to get the best price on your transportation costs. Credit unions often have the best options. Some banks are extremely aggressive. Your auto dealer will work hard for you and provide you with some real good alternatives. Just remember, it is best *not* to have your money invested in a car. Transportation is an expense that can be controlled.

Step 7

THE GOLDEN MOMENT

The delivery process of a new vehicle is sometimes called the "Golden Moment". In years past, spoiling you or pleasing you was often overlooked by the dealer. The customers didn't know any differently, they had always been treated this way. Dealers treated you as prey, not as customers!

You would come out of the business office after signing the papers, the salesman would hand you the keys, you'd get in that shiny, sweet-smelling new vehicle, and proceed to drive away and hope that the nearest gas station was a block or two away or you just might run out of gas. Then, it seems that all gasoline gauges were on "E" or below.

Now, manufacturers reimburse the dealer for a full tank of gas, and now, your salesperson will probably take this opportunity to take you on an orientation drive to get you even better acquainted with your new vehicle and so they can become better acquainted with you. They want your repeat business!

Back then, you had 12 months or 12,000 miles to work the bugs out of your new vehicle. Minor problems that might drive you mad such as squeaks, rattles and adjustments would be repaired at no charge, oftentimes grudgingly, for only 90 days. Now, it's a minimum of 36 months or 36,000 miles bumper-to-bumper. This includes squeaks and rattles.

I think it took the Japanese grabbing a big slice of our market to wake us up and make us realize that you couldn't make it just selling everyone once. Then, in comes the age of *CSI*, *SSI*, *QCP*, or whatever the acronym the manufacturer chose for "Customer Satisfaction". You are expected to respond to a survey to tell the manufacturer how you perceived the dealer, product, and service. It took a while, but many things have changed for the better.

Now, you can expect to begin receiving the *service* you were told you would get. Here are some tips to help you get better service:

1.   Place a call to your salesman to confirm the delivery schedule; it's courteous and smart. I cannot recall how many times I have scheduled an appointment for delivery and the customer shows up a few hours early and can't understand why it takes so long to clean a new vehicle. The *Make-Ready* department personnel do not respond well to pressure. They are usually paid by the hour.

2.   Set aside time to go through the vehicle delivery process at the dealership. Give the dealer at least a couple of hours to talk with you, explain to you, answer any questions you might have and if necessary, drive with you for several miles.

3.   Unless the dealership has a person who performs the

delivery of your vehicle, the salesperson is usually the one responsible. Your salesperson will review with you, your owner's manual, warranty information booklet, and all the other written data that comes with your vehicle. You should then be presented with at least 2 sets of keys as he escorts you on a tour of the dealership facility ending with a visit to the service department. It's a good idea to meet the service write-up person and service manager at this time.

> *The only dumb questions are the ones not asked.*

4. Be sure you know how to operate your new car completely. Take your time; the salesman understands your excitement. It's evident from the wide smile on your face as you slide in behind the wheel. Be certain, at this time, that you carefully inspect your new vehicle both inside and out. Any concerns that you have such as damage to paint or fabric should be noted *in writing* and signed by the sales and/or service manager then and there! Get a copy! Don't hurry and find problems when you get home. A good understanding makes everlasting friends.

It reminds me of the time in 1973 on my third day as being in a command position. I was the used car manager in a small dealership. I was also the only person on the lot.

A couple that appeared to be in their early forties, drove in with a '62 T-Bird that was in mint condition and wanted to trade it on a new car. I loved those cars since I was a kid.

They selected a new LTD then followed me over to their T-Bird for an appraisal. This was such a fine car. I hoped I could give them very little for it so I could buy it for myself.

The man handed me the keys and I unlocked and opened

the driver's door. The car had one of the first *memory seats* that began moving back. The steering wheel was almost in the middle of the car. It was the tilt-away kind that would tilt up and away toward the middle of the car when you opened the door. All you had to do then was to pull it back over once you closed the door and it locked in place.

I pushed the turn signal indicator toward the dash in order to tilt the wheel down. After I had done this and righted the wheel, I glanced at the couple who were frozen, their eyes popped out of their heads. The man jerked the door open and began yelling angrily, "You broke it!" he growled. "Broke what?" I asked. "The steering column!" he hissed. "What are you talking about?" I asked again.

I then proceeded to repeat my steps under their close supervision. They were totally amazed to find out that the steering wheel *tilted* when I pushed the turn signal indicator. The man calmed down quickly and smiled. "Do you know that this has been the most uncomfortable car to drive for the past 11 years," he stated. "I've been driving it with that wheel way up in the air since I bought it. I like the car and I only wanted to trade it because of that damned misplaced steering wheel. Wish you had been around when I first bought it."

He thanked me, got in, repeated what I did and brought the wheel down to where he wanted it, and he and his wife drove off.

Speaking of driving off, now is a good time to discuss "downtime" and a substitute vehicle for transportation and get it in writing. Ask about this *before* you get in the car and drive off.

From the dealer's standpoint, there are three kinds of car buyers:

✿The *nitpicker* is the type who inspects and complains about everything. They will look at their vehicle from all angles looking to see if was wrecked or damaged since they agreed to purchase it. They will run their hands over every square inch of the car to see if the paint has even the tiniest lump. They look at the tires, maybe even kick them. They inspect every piece of fabric and stitch in the upholstery, check to see if the tire tools are in the trunk compartment, click on each light, push every button and twist every knob. They will turn on the windshield wipers, run each window up and down—*everything*! They are the car salesman/dealers nightmare!

The fact is, some of this isn't all bad. I've seen dealerships send a car off without a spare tire. Since it's hidden under the trunk floor, people "assume" it's there. Same with the tools. A tire is useless without the specialized tools it takes to change a flat. And there are many instances that a car that is ordered will get a dent here or there *en route* to the dealership. Then there's . . .

✿The *anxious* type, who just gets in and drives off. They are so busy that they won't even take the sincere kindness and concern of the salesperson; they can read the booklet at home. If not, they will call back and find out how to operate this or that.

This isn't to say that this type is so bad, it's just that a "little" checking and "some" instruction is truly necessary. It's much easier to have these various "things" demonstrated by the salesperson while you are there looking rather than try to explain a problem over the phone or pulling in a gas station and not know how to open the gas tank cover or how to raise the hood. Ultimately, they have to come back for an orientation. Then there's . . .

✿The *ideal car buyer*, who asks for help in such a nice way that dealers and salespeople are happy to go above and beyond to see that things are done quickly and carefully for them. You really do catch more flies with sugar than you do with salt. This type makes it an endurable profession to sell cars and deal with the public.

A WISE STATEMENT

Know also that you have purchased a mass-produced vehicle and it might not ever be perfect. Your manufacturer's warranty should cover the cost to repair defects in materials and workmanship.

Consider *not* having a little bump in the paint repaired. It happens on many cars and in a week or two, even with careful driving, you'll have a ding or two (or 10) that will look far worse than that little "bump" in the paint that the *nitpicker* feels when he runs his hands over the car.

Repainting panels on new vehicles is not uncommon. Be advised that dark colors (black in particular) may look worse than the original defect when repainted. It is extremely difficult if not impossible for even the best body shops to make things perfect.

If you aren't the type to accept a slight imperfection, and you want it corrected, this is probably the *only* opportunity you will have to select a different vehicle! Hopefully, your new vehicle will be flawless and if not, change it! I want you to be satisfied. The dealership exists on the fact that you are.

This brings to mind a rather bizarre story that happened to me several years ago when I sold a new truck to a big, burly Redneck. The truck was magnificent. He had every option in stock added. I remember it well; it was shiny black and lots of chrome.

Once the deal was made, we brought the truck to him in the driveway of the dealership. His wife had dropped him off and was waiting in her car until he got the keys to his new truck and followed her home.

We were ready to start our goodby waves when he got out of the truck, went to his wife's car, signaled for her to hit the trunk latch and he came back to his beautiful new truck with a hammer. He stopped at the right side of the tailgate where he proceeded to raise the hammer high overhead and let it come crashing down. . .WHAM! The sales manager, used car manager and I stood there, mouths agape, our eyes frozen open, in utter astonishment.

Calmly and without emotion, the Redneck turned, walked back to his wife's car, put the hammer back, closed the trunk lid, walked to his new truck and got in. As he was about to drive off, I motioned for him to roll the window down. I asked him why he did that to his new truck.

He spit out a wad of chewing tobacco and said, "I'd kill the sonofabitch who put the first dent in my beautiful, new truck. With my size and temper, I figure I just saved somebody's life!"

With that story behind us, I want to say that this ends what I can tell you about buying a new car, what to do, what to expect, what to demand, what to pass over and what to plan on. It was my life for over 20 years and there were good times and bad times, mostly good.

I hope I didn't paint a dark picture of car dealers or car salespeople because they are just like you; they just happen to be in the business of selling. I want this book to make you fully aware of how it's done and how to make the best deal on a new car that is possible. You can, if you read this book and if you follow the charts I've outlined.

It will take some time and research to car shop the way I suggest. But, if you want to save a *lot* of money on your next new car purchase, there are few shortcuts. I want you to have a new car and I want you to get a deal on one. Good luck and may God bless you!

Buckle Up   Drive Carefully   Be Happy

NOTES

NOTES

OTHER BOOKS BY SWAN PUBLISHING

HOW NOT TO BE LONELY . . . If you're about to marry, recently divorced or widowed, want to forgive, forget or both, this is an excellent book to read. Candid, positive, entertaining and informative. If you're looking for a new person, this tells **where** to find them, **what** to say and **how to keep them** once you get them. (over 2 million copies sold) . . . . $ 9.95

HOW NOT TO BE LONELY <u>TONIGHT</u> . . . Aimed at the *MALE* reader. Other than being courageous and strong, smart women want their man to be sensitive, caring, and understanding. "The" book to give to your man. Or, for men who really want to learn what turns the modern woman on. A fun book for your coffee table . . . . $ 9.95

NEW FATHER'S BABY GUIDE . . . The "perfect" gift for ALL new fathers. Orientates dad about Lamaze classes, burping, feeding and changing the baby plus 40 side-splitting drawings. Most of all, it tells dad how to **SPOIL** mom! Mothers, sisters, girlfriends, grandmothers, **get this book for dad, he needs it!** . . . $ 9.95

YOUR FRONT YARD . . . A fun book of information by garden expert John Burrow. It tells about plants, trees, grass, pesticides, fertilizer, lawn and garden maintenance, **everything** you need to know to plant or keep a beautiful front yard . . . . $ 9.95

VEGETABLE GARDENING *(Spring and Fall)* . . . Another fine, fun book written by John Burrow. It tells the size garden you need to feed your family, which vegetables grow best for a country, city, and even an apartment garden on your patio or in planters, *plus*, all about herb gardens to impress your friends . . . $ 9.95

REVERSING IMPOTENCE FOREVER . . . Written by Dr. David Mobley and Dr. Steven Wilson, world renowned urologists, who specialize in impotence . This book tells it **all**, and includes diagrams as well as numbers to call for additional information and/or help. It *can* change your sex life for the better. **Women** buy this book 50 to 1 over men. Men, find out what you need to know . . . . $ 9.95

QUEST FOR MEGALODON . . . An adventure book written by ocean-engineer, Tom Dade, about a supposedly extinct shark that ruled the oceans more than 50 million years ago. A physician, a Hall of Fame baseball player and an oceanographer, once boyhood fishing buddies, reunite for the adventure of a lifetime. *JAWS* was 20 feet long and weighed 3 tons. Megalodon is **100** feet long and weighs **60** tons! (About to be made into a movie) . . . . $ 9.95

HOME IMPROVEMENT . . . *Homeowner's Most Often Asked Questions,* written by Tom Tynan, tells how to repair plumbing, fix leaky toilets, paint cabinets, install tile, put in light fixtures, how to choose a repairmen, paint certain woods, check air conditioner, install insulation, handle roof problems, etc. A truly excellent book on home repair that will save you $$$. . . . .$ 9.95

BUILDING & REMODELING, *A Homeowner's Guide To Getting Started.* Another Tom Tynan book that tells if **you** should do it, or how to hire a contractor to do it for you. Explains financing, plans, inspections—everything you need to know. . . . . $ 9.95

BUYING & SELLING A HOME, *A Homeowner's Guide To Survival,* for the person buying or selling a home. Talks about agents, loans, what to fix up, what not to, what to look for, moving, location; inspectors, laws—everything! Realtors buy this book and marvel at the information . . . . $ 9.95

CLIFF EVANS is available for personal appearances, luncheons, banquets, interviews, seminars, etc. He is entertaining and informative. Call **(713) 388-2547** for cost and availability.

☆ ☆ ☆ ☆ ☆ ☆

Send a personal check or money order in the amount of $12.85 per copy to: Swan Publishing, 126 Live Oak, Alvin, TX, 77511. Please allow 7-10 days for delivery.

☆ ☆ ☆ ☆ ☆ ☆

To order by major credit card 24 hours a day call: **(713) 268-6776** or long distance **1-800-866-8961.**

☆ ☆ ☆ ☆ ☆ ☆

Libraries—Bookstores—Quantity Orders:

Swan Publishing
126 Live Oak
Alvin, TX 77511

Call **(713) 388-2547**
FAX **(713) 585-3738**